Animals
KRUGER
OF THE NATIONAL
PARK

G. DE GRAAFF

Centre for Wildlife Research, University of Pretoria

This book has been produced by Struik Publishers, Cape Town, in collaboration
with the National Parks Board of Trustees, Pretoria.

ACKNOWLEDGEMENTS

I would like to thank the National Parks Board for the opportunities and facilities granted to me while compiling this text. I am also grateful to the photographers who provided the excellent illustrations which accompany the text.
The animals of the Kruger National Park have been studied over the years by several outstanding biologists, including Dr U. de V. Pienaar, Dr S.C.J. Joubert, Dr A.C. Kemp, Ken Newman, Prof. G.L. Maclean and the late Dr R.H.N. Smithers. I have made full use of their findings in preparing this book.
I also acknowledge the help I received during the preparation of this book from Mrs J.C. (Kobie) Rautenbach and Mrs J.E. (Joanita) Fourie (both colleagues in the former Department of Research and Information) who respectively typed and edited the manuscript with efficiency. Finally, to all at Struik Publishers, a warm word of thanks for their effective guidance.

G. de Graaff
Pretoria, 1992

Struik Publishers
(a member of The Struik Group (Pty) Ltd)
Cornelis Struik House
80 McKenzie Street
Cape Town
8001

Reg. No. 63/00203/07

First published 1987
Second edition 1992
Copyright © text: G. de Graaff 1987, 1992

Photographic credits
The names of the individual photographers appear alongside their respective images. Copyright © rests with the photographers and/or their appointed agents.

Edited by: Nicola Marshall, Cape Town
Design and DTP make up: Tamsyn Ivey, Cape Town
Reproduction by: Unifoto (Pty) Ltd, Cape Town
Printed and bound by: National Book Printers, Goodwood

ISBN 1 86825 283 3

INTRODUCTION

The Kruger National Park is situated in the tropical and subtropical Lowveld of the north-eastern and eastern Transvaal, lying between 22°10' and 25°32'S and between 30°50' and 32°02'E. It forms part of the Southern Savanna Woodland biotic zone of sub-Saharan Africa – a zone now increasingly under threat from unrestricted human population growth and consequent habitat destruction.

With an area of 19 485 square kilometres, the Park is larger than the state of Israel, about the same size as Wales and about two-thirds the size of Belgium. It is one of only 14 national parks in the world more than 15 000 square kilometres in extent. Bordering on Zimbabwe to the north and Mozambique to the east, the Park stretches 320 kilometres from north to south and 65 kilometres from east to west at its widest part.

The Park is internationally famous as a wildlife sanctuary and is home to at least 147 mammal, 507 bird, 114 reptile, 33 amphibian and 49 freshwater fish species. The Park's insect fauna is abundant, and has recently been documented by Braack (Struik 1991). In one well-recorded group, the butterflies, at least 227 species have been recorded. Botanically the Kruger National Park is no less rich, with a total of 1 986 species of plants recorded to date, 457 of these being trees and shrubs and 235 being grasses.

Every year, many thousands of tourists (700 000 in 1991) visit the Kruger National Park, attracted by the magnificence of its wildlife. The vastness of the area is an added attraction as vistors can see and experience wild animals roaming freely in their natural habitat without a fence in sight.

This book was compiled to help visitors explore and enjoy to the utmost the wildlife experience that the Park provides. It presents information on 51 mammal, 126 bird and 11 reptile species. All are of common occurrence, or are at least highly visible inhabitants of the bushveld, and are those which I believe the average tourist has a fair chance of seeing during a visit lasting two or three days.

Try to get to know the animals you are likely to see in the Park, as studying animals in their natural settings can be difficult and is often tedious. Most fail to appear when you want to see them, or appear suddenly only to disappear as quickly, allowing you little time for observation.

However, learning to observe is the first step towards enjoying them. Start with the species that frequent the rest-camp grounds – a bird, a lizard or a squirrel. Take a closer look at those species frequenting the side of the road – impala, baboon or giraffe. If an animal has disappeared into a burrow, remain stationary and quiet: usually it will reappear to find out where you are and what you are doing. Look out for evidence of animal activities such as shelters, nests, trails in the grass, piles of dung or tracks along the road.

Decide on what you want to see and concentrate on areas where the species of your choice is likely to occur. When travelling by car, do so at a speed well below the official speed limit. You can miss a surprising amount of biological activity if you drive too fast. The hot, midday hours are not very productive; animals are often immobile and camouflaged when standing or lying down in the shade of trees. Look for animals during the early hours of the morning (up to 10:00) and again during the later afternoon (from 15:30 onwards). Interaction between species is often seen to best advantage at a water-hole. You need patience, but several species often come down to drink simultaneously and a wide variety of game can be seen within a short space of time.

As your powers of observation improve, try to assess where an animal fits into the process known as a 'food-chain'. There are hundreds of such chains in any natural environment but they all function in the same way. As they grow, plants store the sun's energy in their leaves, buds and other growing tissues. A plant is therefore referred to as a 'primary producer', to use the jargon of the ecologist. By eating a part of a plant, an animal acquires this stored energy. Such an animal becomes a 'primary consumer'. When the primary consumer is eaten, the energy in its tissues, which is already diminished in amount, is acquired by the predator that ate it. Such an animal is called a 'secondary consumer'. The process continues until there is no predator capable of killing and eating the ultimate possessor of the primary producer's stored energy – now much reduced. The apex of the food-chain has been reached. The eventual death of the animal at the top of the chain returns the remaining energy to lesser life-forms. Parts of the dead animal may furnish a meal for a carrion-eater, some may be consumed by insect larvae while the rest of the body is returned to the soil where it is processed and broken down by fungi, bacteria and other micro-organisms. Now the cycle can begin again. Remember that while some participants in the food-chain may appear unpleasant, all have a role to play in the health of the Park's ecosystems. The message is clear: if you really want to understand the animals in the Kruger National Park you must try to understand something of the complex relationships that exist between them and their near neighbours in the wildlife community.

Please bear in mind that this part of the world belongs to the plants and the animals and that we have entered their domain as visitors. If we understand them, we will learn to be considerate to their needs and they will continue to thrive in their wilderness surroundings. Observe, enjoy and appreciate the animals, but do not disturb them.

This book is not intended to be a complete guide to the species discussed within its covers. Instead, I have attempted to capture something of the spirit of the wild creatures I have encountered over the past 30 years, and in this way I pay tribute to them and to the national park that has sustained them so wonderfully since its foundation in 1898.

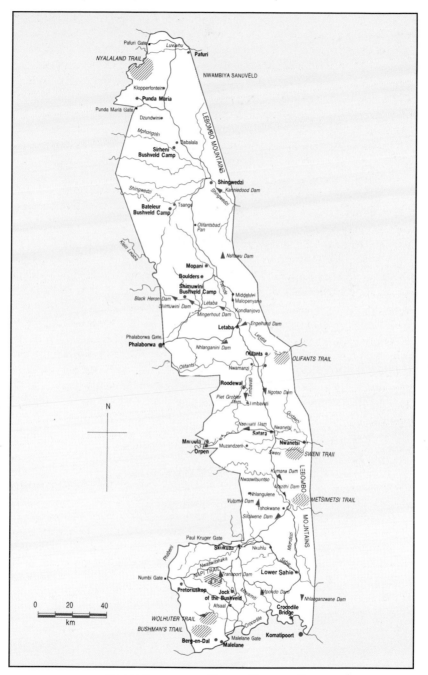

VISITORS' MAP TO THE KRUGER NATIONAL PARK

5

BLACK RHINOCEROS

BLACK RHINOCEROS

Diceros bicornis

SWARTRENOSTER

The black rhinoceros is smaller than the white rhinoceros, from which it may be distinguished by its prehensile, 'hooked' upper lip, which is adapted for browsing. It carries its head higher than the white rhinoceros, which has a 'squared' upper lip, and has no hump on its neck. The record length for a front horn in southern Africa is 1,05 metres. Adult males stand approximately 160 centimetres at the shoulder and can attain a mass of just over 1 000 kilograms.

Calves may be born in any month of the year, after a gestation period of 15 months; at birth they have a mass of between 30 and 40 kilograms. In contrast to the white rhino, the black rhino calf usually canters alongside or just behind its mother. Black rhinos are less sociable than white rhinos, the only stable bond being that between the cow and her calf. They are also inclined to be irritable and bad-tempered and will readily attack people whether they are on foot or in vehicles.

In the Lowveld the black rhinoceros withstood man's onslaught better than the white rhinoceros. However, while in 1936 there were still solitary specimens in the dense Nwatimiri Wood some 18 kilometres west of Lower Sabie, it became extinct in the Kruger National Park shortly afterwards.

In co-operation with the Natal Parks Board, however, two individuals were re-introduced on 17 May 1971 and released near Skukuza. These were soon followed by further batches of black rhino from Natal and Zimbabwe. This exercise has been so successful that there are currently more than 150 black rhinoceros in the Park.

WHITE RHINOCEROS

WHITE RHINOCEROS

Ceratotherium simum

WITRENOSTER

The white rhinoceros is Africa's second-largest land mammal after the elephant. Bulls can attain a shoulder height of over 180 centimetres with a mass of around 2 800 kilograms. It is more than twice as heavy as its cousin the black rhinoceros, from which it may be distinguished by its broad muzzle with a 'squared' upper lip, which is adapted for grazing.

Indiscriminate hunting eradicated the white rhinoceros from the Lowveld towards the end of the 19th century. The species was reintroduced to the Kruger National Park on 13 October 1961 when four adults were transported from the Umfolozi Game Reserve in Natal to the Pretoriuskop area. This small population, helped by further introductions, grew steadily and by 1991 it was estimated that there were 1 381 white rhinoceros in the Park – the largest single population of this species in Africa.

The gestation period in the white rhino is about 16 months and a single calf is born with a mass of about 40 kilograms. There is no fixed breeding season. While still dependent on its mother, the calf usually ambles ahead of her – unlike the black rhinoceros calf which travels alongside or behind its mother. Again unlike the black rhinoceros, the white rhino is fairly placid and would rather move away from interference or trouble than attack. It is also more sociable in its relations with others of its own species.

Males establish territories which they defend against other high-ranking bulls. Several cows and their calves, and even subordinate bulls, will share a bull's territory and sometimes those of adjacent bulls.

PHOTO ACCESS/DAVID STEELE

AFRICAN ELEPHANTS

AFRICAN ELEPHANT
Loxodonta africana
AFRIKA-OLIFANT

Elephants were hunted mercilessly in the Transvaal Lowveld during the late 19th century, and by 1912 only an estimated 25 survived – in the Olifants Gorge area near the present-day Olifants Rest Camp. This nucleus herd reacted favourably to the sanctuary afforded it by the Sabie Game Reserve and, supplemented by immigrating elephants from across the Mozambique border, the elephant population had increased to about 100 by 1926 when the Reserve was formally reproclaimed as the Kruger National Park.

Elephants consume impressive quantities of food – between 150 and 300 kilograms daily – and if they have free access to water may drink as much as 180 to 220 litres a day. It is not surprising, therefore, that an adult elephant can produce between 140 and 180 kilograms of dung in a 24-hour period. They also eat a wider variety of plants than any other herbivore in the Park and they spend much of their time foraging. Clearly, large populations of elephants can alter or damage the habitat significantly by their feeding methods and for this reason elephant numbers within the Park have to be controlled. Today elephants are studied by scientists to determine just how to manage their numbers for the long-term benefit both of the elephants and of the Kruger National Park itself.

The 1990 census revealed 7 278 animals, comprising 1 199 bulls and 6 079 animals in breeding herds (including 145 calves under one year of age). Park managers have determined the elephant's population 'ceiling' at 7 000 to 8 000 animals.

BURCHELL'S ZEBRA

BURCHELL'S ZEBRA
Equus burchellii
BONTSEBRA

With its distinctive black-and-white striped coat, the zebra is a very well-known animal and needs no introduction to the general public. But although all zebra may look alike at first sight, close inspection reveals that no two animals are identical. Burchell's zebra, which is also known as the plains zebra, has greyish 'shadow' stripes between the black ones on the hindquarters; the mountain zebra, South Africa's other zebra species, has no shadow stripes. The adult stallions have a shoulder height of about 140 centimetres, and may have a mass of up to 320 kilograms.

Burchell's zebra is a typical savanna species, favouring open areas and avoiding forests and deserts; it is very adaptable to changing environments. It is highly gregarious and forms aggregations of thousands of animals when conditions are suitable. It is often seen in the company of other plains game, particularly blue wildebeest.

Burchell's zebra is primarily a grazer but occasionally browses on herbs and shrubs. Foaling occurs throughout the year, but in the Park there is a definite peak in December and January. The gestation lasts some 360 to 390 days, and a single foal weighing about 30 kilograms is born. The bond between mother and foal is very close, especially during the first three or four days.

The aerial census which took place between May and September 1990 has a count of 31 910 zebra within the Park's boundaries, excluding the Punda Maria area. After the impala and the buffalo, this species is the most abundant herbivore in the Kruger National Park.

PHOTO ACCESS/LEX HES

HIPPOPOTAMUS

HIPPOPOTAMUS
Hippopotamus amphibius
SEEKOEI

The hippopotamus is so well known that a description of its general appearance is unnecessary. Nevertheless, a few points arising from its amphibious mode of life are worth mentioning. The hippo is in fact an excellent and graceful swimmer, no matter how ungainly it may appear on land. It has several interesting adaptations which equip it for a semi-aquatic existence, for example nostrils and ears which can be closed off when submerging.

The skin of the hippo is of special interest. It is virtually hairless, has no sweat-glands and has an unusually thin epidermis over a thick dermis. This latter feature means that in dry air the hippo's rate of water loss is several times that of other mammals – therefore it needs to resort to deep water during the heat of the day in order to avoid possible dehydration.

The hippopotamus does, however, possess specialized skin-glands which secrete a viscous reddish fluid – the source of the misconception that the hippo 'sweats blood'. The red colour is caused by skin pigments which are resistant to ultraviolet radiation and thereby protect the skin from the ravages of sunburn.

The bull can exceed 1 500 kilograms in mass and it stands 150 centimetres tall at the shoulder.

The 1990 census revealed an estimated 2 575 hippos in the Park. Of these, 181 were counted in dams and pools away from the rivers, 306 were in the Crocodile River, 725 in the Sabie, 611 in the Olifants, 686 in the Letaba and 66 in the Luvuvhu and Limpopo combined.

WARTHOG

WARTHOG
Phacochoerus aethiopicus
VLAKVARK

Although Theodore Roosevelt was not alone in expressing the opinion that warthogs 'are hideous beasts, with strange protuberances on their cheeks', it has to be said that anything warthogs may lack in grace and beauty is more than made up for in power, adaptability and intelligence. Warthogs occur throughout the Park and are particularly abundant in the Lower Sabie/Crocodile Bridge area, around Orpen and Tshokwane, and in the far north between the Luvuvhu and Limpopo rivers. In 1990 there were an estimated 2 715 of these animals in the Park.

Warthogs are active by day and are semi-gregarious. Family groups usually comprise a mature sow with her most recent piglets, sometimes accompanied by the boar. For most of the year the latter lives alone or in a bachelor group. Home ranges overlap and the boars are polygamous. Fighting for dominance and mating rights during the short mating season in April and May involves pushing contests in which boars slash at each other with their tusks (up to 60 centimetres long). Injuries to the face are minimized by the presence of two pairs of large 'warts' below the eyes and on the cheeks; sows, incidentally, have only one pair of warts which are situated just below the eyes and which are much smaller than those of the males.

At night warthogs sleep in burrows or holes, entering the cavity backwards so that they can face any intruder. Sows also farrow in a burrow after a gestation period of about 170 days, their litters averaging from two to three piglets.

GIRAFFE

GIRAFFE
Giraffa camelopardalis
KAMEELPERD

An unmistakable and typical animal of the African savanna, the giraffe is the tallest living animal with bulls attaining head heights of over 5 metres. In 1990 there were an estimated 4 719 giraffes in the Kruger National Park, the highest concentrations being found between the Sabie and Olifants rivers.

Scientists have long been intrigued by the giraffe's ability to control its blood pressure; when a giraffe bends its head to drink, one would expect there to be a sudden alteration in blood pressure as the head moves from a point three metres above the heart to a point two metres below the heart – at one moment the heart is pumping against gravity, and the next moment it is pumping with gravity. The reverse of course applies to venous blood returning to the heart.

The giraffe has in fact developed special adaptations to cope with these problems. As in other ungulates, the blood vessels which feed the brain (the common carotid and the external carotid arteries) each divide into a tight network of small vessels, the rete mirabile, before entering the brain; in the giraffe, however, the small vessels of the rete mirabile have very elastic walls which can accommodate excess blood when the head is lowered and thus prevent the brain from being flooded. When the giraffe returns to its normal upright position, the rete retains enough blood to feed the brain for the few moments it takes the heart to readjust to the new situation. The problem of fluctuating venous pressures is solved by a unique system of valves in the larger veins which prevents backflow.

CAPE BUFFALO BULL

CAPE BUFFALO
Syncerus caffer
KAAPSE BUFFEL

The buffalo is extremely adaptable and can be found in virtually all the habitats in the Park. Primarily a grazer, it is sensitive to heat so most of its foraging is carried out at night, the daylight hours being used for resting and ruminating in the shade. The buffalo has poor eyesight and hearing but its sense of smell is well developed.

Buffalo are gregarious, occurring in herds ranging from a few individuals to several hundred animals. They are not territorial and in hard times will leave their normal home range in search of better feeding conditions. Old bulls often leave the herds and live alone or in small groups, especially among the reeds of river-beds. Although peaceful in their relations with their own kind, buffalo are temperamental beasts and in certain circumstances can be aggressive and formidable fighters. Wounded buffalo have been known to wait in ambush for, and even to stalk, pursuing hunters and are reputed to be the most dangerous of big game animals to hunt.

Buffalo are susceptible to disease and the great rinderpest epidemic of 1896/97 all but exterminated them. They are vulnerable to foot-and-mouth disease: this viral disease does not necessarily kill buffalo but it does weaken them and they may then succumb to other infections or to predation.

To prevent habitat damage, Park authorities cull considerable numbers of buffalo each year. According to the 1990 census there were at least 27 857 buffalo in the Kruger National Park, of which 25 738 were in breeding herds and 2 119 were bachelor bulls.

NYALA BULL

NYALA EWE

NYALA

Tragelaphus angasii

NJALA

The nyala is one of the less common antelope species of the Kruger National Park, and certainly one of the most attractive. It prefers thickets in dry savanna woodland and in the Park is especially common in the river-bank vegetation of the Luvuvhu and Limpopo rivers. It is a semi-gregarious species and can be found in herds of as many as 30 animals, although smaller groups of up to five individuals are most common. These smaller groups normally consist of females and their young, with the males tending to be solitary or in small bachelor groups. Males join the groups of females and young opportunely at favoured feeding or watering sites, or when one of the females is receptive to mating.

The nyala is notably sexually dimorphic, that is, the males and females are markedly different in appearance. This is not simply because only the males have horns, but because there is a remarkable difference in size, coat colour and hair length between the sexes. The males are larger, measuring 112 centimetres at the shoulder, with an average mass of 108 kilograms, and are dark brown or grey in colour and shaggier. The females are smaller with a height of 97 centimetres, weigh 62 kilograms on average, and are bright orange-brown in colour, and short-haired. The nyala's diet varies in accordance with what food is available, and it will take both graze and browse.

The nyala's preference for thickets and closed woodland makes it a difficult animal to census. In 1985 scientists counted 318 individuals in the Kruger National Park, but this was certainly an underestimate.

KUDU BULL

KUDU COW

KUDU

Tragelaphus strepsiceros

KOEDOE

To many people the kudu bull with its magnificent corkscrew-shaped large horns is the most handsome of all antelope. The kudu is a large, fairly timid animal with a distinctive white chevron-shaped mark extending from the eyes across the upper nose. It has disproportionately large ears and only the males have horns. The male is larger than the female: it has a shoulder height of around 140 centimetres and a mass of 250 kilograms compared with the female's height of 125 centimetres and mass of 160 kilograms.

The kudu is the most widely distributed antelope species in the Park, inhabiting all the different habitat types, albeit in different densities. It is, however, particularly partial to rugged, broken country where sufficient thicket for shelter is available. Of all southern African bovids, the kudu is the least selective as far as food plants are concerned. At least 148 different species of plant have been identified in its diet in the Park, and although it is essentially a browser, it will on occasion eat fresh green grass.

Kudu are semi-gregarious, associating in family groups of five to 10 individuals, although larger groups are not uncommon. Outside the rutting season, bulls tend to be solitary or to form small bachelor groups. While aggression among bulls is infrequent, they engage in 'pushing duels' which are contests of strength to establish dominance. Kudu are susceptible to epizootic diseases such as rinderpest and anthrax.

Slightly more than 7 000 kudu were counted in the Kruger National Park in the 1990 census.

BUSHBUCK RAM

BUSHBUCK EWE

BUSHBUCK

Tragelaphus scriptus
BOSBOK

The bushbuck is a small- to medium-sized antelope, with adult males standing about 80 centimetres high at the shoulder. The females are slightly smaller with a shoulder height of 70 centimetres. Only the males have horns, which may attain a length of 50 centimetres.

Coat colour and markings vary greatly from area to area and the subspecies that is found in the Transvaal Lowveld tends to be intermediate between the southern Cape bushbuck (which lacks white body stripes) and the Chobe bushbuck of Botswana and the Zambezi drainage (which is well marked with white stripes and spots).

These graceful animals are often seen singly, but they also occur in pairs or small family groups. They generally lie up in dense undergrowth of forest and riverine thicket during the day and emerge to feed during the late afternoon, the night and early morning. Although predominantly browsers, they will also take young grass-shoots when available.

Bushbuck are tolerant towards one another and even mild forms of aggression are rare. Despite their shy and retiring habits, however, they can be extremely pugnacious if attacked, cornered or wounded.

The ewe gives birth to a single offspring after a gestation period of some six months. These may be born at any time of the year, but mostly during October and November in the Park. The lambs are hidden away in the days following birth until they are strong enough to join their mothers.

Although bushbuck are difficult to census, there are an estimated 1 200 in the Park.

IMPALA RAMS

IMPALA

Aepyceros melampus
ROOIBOK

The impala is the most abundant antelope species in the Kruger National Park, with 116 223 individuals recorded during the 1990 census. Highly gregarious, it occurs in small herds of from 10 to 50 animals. The greatest concentrations of impala in the Park are to be found in the area south of the Olifants River and north of the Sabie River, where in 1985 biologists recorded 48 herds each over 100 strong, along with numerous smaller groupings.

Only the males have horns, which are lyre-shaped and strongly ringed for two-thirds of their length. Rams have a shoulder height of around 90 centimetres and an average mass of 50 kilograms. They are extraordinarily fleet-footed, and when alarmed can execute a series of graceful leaps, each one of which may carry them in excess of 10 metres. Despite their agility, their large numbers and convenient size ensure for them an important place in the diet of all the larger predators.

They favour habitats along the perennial rivers where water is freely available, the grass is short, and where there are medium to dense stands of shrubs. They will take both browse and grass.

The impala's mating season is restricted to the autumn months of April, May and June. At this time the rams establish territories and attempt to gather 'harems' of ewes and their young. One adult male accompanies each female herd, and he is constantly engaged in defending his harem and fighting off challengers. Ewes do not respect the territorial boundaries set by the rams, who have to work hard to retain their ewes.

WATERBUCK

WATERBUCK

Kobus ellipsiprymnus

WATERBOK

Waterbuck are large, thickset antelopes, the males standing about 170 centimetres at the shoulder and having a mass of as much as 270 kilograms. Their overall colour is dark brownish-grey, with a grizzled appearance imparted by white and grey hairs. Perhaps their most distinctive feature, however, is the broad white ring encircling the tail on the buttocks. Waterbuck hair is coarse and somewhat shaggy, especially on the neck and upper breast. Only the males have horns, slightly lyre-shaped and curving backwards, upwards and then slightly forwards at the tip.

The waterbuck is endowed with numerous glands over its body, which produce a secretion with a musky goat-like smell. This secretion is presumed to have a water-proofing function although it has also been suggested that it acts as an insect repellent. It is a gregarious species and is always found near water in open bush country. Although herds of from 30 to 60 animals may be encountered, in the Park the most frequent group size is between six and 12 animals. Cows and young predominate in the larger herds which are led by a mature bull. They are primarily grazers, but will occasionally take browse.

Waterbuck wade readily in shallow water, especially when they are drinking, and are good swimmers; when in danger they are known to seek sanctuary in deeper water where pursuers – particularly wild dogs – are reluctant to follow.

According to the 1990 census figures, the total of waterbuck in the Kruger National Park is in the order of 3 200 animals.

REEDBUCK RAM AND EWE

REEDBUCK
Redunca arundinum
RIETBOK

The reedbuck, as its name suggests, is associated with marshy or riverine situations where reeds can be found. It must also, however, have access to stands of tall grass both for cover and for grazing. Although it avoids woodland and scrub, it will tolerate scattered trees and shrubs within its grassland habitat.

Only the male reedbuck carries horns, which curve gently forwards and are ridged or corrugated transversely for two-thirds of their length. When danger threatens, the reedbuck will freeze and is difficult to see. On the other hand, when it is alarmed enough to take to flight it is very noticeable, flashing the conspicuous white underside of its bushy tail and snorting loudly.

In some populations of reedbuck, such as that in the Kruger National Park, a black glandular patch can often be seen near the base of the ear.

Reedbuck are semi-gregarious and may be seen singly, in pairs or in small family groups. In the dry winter months, however, larger associations of up to 20 animals can be seen. A reedbuck male will establish a territory some 40 to 60 hectares in extent and protects his ewe from rivals. Lambs can be born at any time of the year although in the Park there seems to be a peak from December to May. The lamb is hidden for the first two months of its life.

In 1963 it was estimated that there were 850 to 900 reedbuck in the Park; the 1985 census indicated that there were about 2 000. They are abundant in suitable habitat throughout the Park, especially in the area between Malelane and Pretoriuskop.

BLUE WILDEBEEST

BLUE WILDEBEEST

Connochaetes taurinus

BLOUWILDEBEES

The blue wildebeest is an ungainly animal with a lugubrious facial appearance. It has a plodding gait which gives the impression of world-weariness, but it is capable of extremely energetic posturings, particularly in the mating season. In this respect it is only slightly less flamboyant than its cousin the black wildebeest, often called 'the clown of the veld'.

It is a large antelope, males having a mass of about 250 kilograms and a shoulder height of 150 centimetres. Both males and females have horns, but those of the female are lighter in build than those of the male.

The blue wildebeest feeds exclusively on graze. It is extremely gregarious, occurring in herds of 20 to 30 and at times congreg-ating in thousands. In the Serengeti Plains of East Africa herds of up to 400 000 have been recorded. Its social organization is fluid outside the rutting season, which in the Kruger National Park occurs in the autumn months of April and May. The bulls then establish territories, round up 'harem' herds of cows and their young and fend off rivals by means of display or horn-sparring contests. Wildebeest calves can stand within three to five minutes of birth, and are able to run with the mother imme-diately thereafter.

An observer approaching a large herd of wildebeest may be able to detect a tar-like smell. This comes from the secretions of glands on the forefeet and on the face just below the eyes; these secretions are used to mark territories and paths.

The 1990 census indicated that the Park contains about 14 300 blue wildebeest.

TSESSEBE

TSESSEBE

Damaliscus lunatus

BASTERHARTBEES

The tsessebe is a large antelope related to the blesbok and the hartebeest. Males attain a mass of around 140 kilograms and have a shoulder height of 120 centimetres. Both sexes possess horns.

The habitat requirements of tsessebe include availability of water and medium to tall grasses in a lightly wooded savanna environment. It avoids trampled areas and dense stands of trees and shrubs. Grass forms the bulk of the tsessebe's diet, with herbaceous plants being taken occasionally but never browse.

Herds of four to 10 animals appear to be the norm in tsessebe society. Each herd is accompanied by a bull, whose territory may be two to four square kilometres in size in the Park. The bulls mark their territories with the secretions of the facial glands below the eyes and those of the interdigital glands between the toes of both fore- and hindfeet. They often stand on termite-heaps or other mounds in order to advertise their possession of a territory.

Tsessebe are seasonal breeders and the majority of the calves are born in October. The calves are unable to walk for some hours after birth, but despite this are not hidden away; as soon as they can, they join their mothers.

Censuses reveal that the tsessebe population of the Park has declined. In the 1985 census 1 163 individuals were counted, but only 711 animals in 1990 (excluding the Punda Maria area). They are especially common on the basalt plains north of the Letaba River and further north to the Shingwedzi River.

PHOTO ACCESS/DAVID STEELE

SABLE ANTELOPE

SABLE ANTELOPE
Hippotragus niger
SWARTWITPENS

This striking antelope is found throughout the Park, except for the south-eastern area between Lower Sabie and Crocodile Bridge. It favours areas with medium to tall grasses in an open savanna woodland environment, preferably near water.

Sable are large antelopes; males attaining a body mass of some 230 to 250 kilograms and a shoulder height of about 135 centimetres. Both sexes possess horns, but the female's are shorter and more slender than the male's. The young are reddish-brown in colour; this develops to dark brown in adult females and black in old bulls.

They live in herds of up to 30 individuals and occasionally more, although in the Park the average herd size is 14. The bulls are territorial and defend their chosen ranges by display, or if necessary by fighting, when the contestants often drop on to their knees and spar with their horns. The female/calf herds occupy home ranges of some 30 square kilometres which overlap with the bull territories. The rut is seasonal, (end of May to July) and single calves are born between January and March.

Habitat fragmentation and destruction outside the Kruger National Park effectively means that the Park is now the key area for the survival of the species in South Africa. The 1985 census indicated that there were some 2 250 sable antelope in the Park. This total included 329 solitary bulls and 1 911 animals which were in breeding herds. Around 460 calves were counted – approximately one-fifth of the entire population. In the 1990 census, some 1 877 individuals were counted.

ROAN ANTELOPE

ROAN ANTELOPE
Hippotragus equinus
BASTERGEMSBOK

The roan antelope is the second-largest antelope in Africa after the eland. Males stand about 140 centimetres tall at the shoulder and may attain a mass in excess of 270 kilograms. Males and females possess backward-curving horns, but those of the female are shorter and more slender.

Like the tsessebe, the roan antelope appears to prefer the basalt plains adjoining the Lebombo range north of the Letaba River where it frequents the lightly-wooded savanna with medium to tall grasses. It is principally a grazer but will take browse when the grass is unpalatable and dry.

The roan is semi-gregarious, forming small herds ranging in size from four to 12 animals. Each herd is accompanied by a single mature bull. Although the roan is not regarded as being a territorial species, its breeding herds do occur in fixed home ranges or 'activity zones' which may be up to 100 square kilometres in extent. They are not seasonal breeders and the single calves may be born in any month of the year, after a gestation period of just over nine months.

Dominant bulls may succeed in dissuading rivals by mere display, but if that fails they will resort to ritualized horn-pushing duels, similar to those of the sable.

Roan antelope are particularly susceptible to anthrax and their numbers in the Park have never been high. In 1985 the total population was estimated at 344 animals of which 121 had been immunized against anthrax by Park authorities. The 1990 census revealed some 167 animals, evidence of the population decline recorded since 1986.

PETER PICKFORD

KLIPSPRINGER RAM

COMMON DUIKER EWE

KLIPSPRINGER
Oreotragus oreotragus
KLIPSPRINGER

The Afrikaans common name klipspringer, meaning 'rock-jumper', is entirely appropriate for this sure-footed small antelope as it is confined to rocky hills, gorges and koppies. It is widely distributed in the Kruger National Park, occurring wherever suitable rocky habitat is available. The klipspringer's hoofs are specially adapted for this type of rugged environment and it can scamper up rock-faces that are virtually vertical and leap distances of more than six metres from rock to rock. It may often be seen standing motionless on a rock outcrop in characteristic klipspringer fashion with all four feet placed close together.

The klipspringer is territorial and it occurs singly, in pairs or in small family groups. Only the ram has horns and he marks his territory by creating dung-heaps and by rubbing the black sticky secretion of the pre-orbital glands (below the eyes) on to twigs. The adult male stands 60 centimetres at the shoulder and has a mass of about 10 kilograms.

COMMON DUIKER
Sylvicapra grimmia
GEWONE DUIKER

Of the 16 duiker species found in Africa, 15 are elusive forest-dwelling forms. The 16th is the aptly named common duiker which is the only member of the group typically found in savanna and open bush country. Not only is it widespread and common throughout the Kruger National Park, but it is also perhaps the most widely distributed antelope in Africa, occurring from the southern fringes of the Sahara southwards through the savanna zone to the Cape. It has the largest brain mass relative to body size of all antelope.

Duikers avoid both dense forest and open plains and prefer an environment with cover in the form of bushes and thickets. They are shy and secretive creatures and emerge to feed during the late afternoon (extending into the early hours of the night) and in the early morning. They are normally solitary but mother/young pairs are occasionally seen. Females are slightly larger than the males, and only the males have horns.

STEENBOK

Raphicerus campestris
STEENBOK

The steenbok is a small, graceful antelope about 52 centimetres in shoulder height, reddish-brown in colour above and with white underparts. Only the males have horns, which are widely spaced and grow vertically upwards with a very slight forward curve towards the tips. It is generally distributed throughout the Kruger National Park especially in open country where medium and tall grasses are interspersed with patches of shorter grass; it avoids woodland and dense thickets and also extensive areas of short grass.

Oribi and steenbok are often confused in the field but may readily be distinguished by their tail coloration: the upper surface of the steenbok's tail is the same reddish-brown as its body, while the upper surface of the oribi's tail is black.

Steenbok have well-developed glands for scent-marking: these are situated below the eyes, on all four hoofs and, somewhat unusually, between the two halves of the lower jaw. The latter appears to be the most frequently used for scent-marking, on twigs, grass stubble or other objects. They are solitary animals, and both males and females occupy their own individual territories, some 30 hectares in extent. These are defined by scent-marking and by regularly used 'latrine' areas.

They are normally most active from early to mid-morning and again in the late afternoon. In the Park they tend to browse rather than graze and they select plant material of high nutritive value such as young green leaves, soft twigs, buds, fruit and grass shoots.

SHARPE'S GRYSBOK

Raphicerus sharpei

SHARPE-GRYSBOK

Sharpe's grysbok is a small antelope standing about 45 centimetres at the shoulder and with a mass of around 7,5 kilograms. Only the males possess horns. It is closely related to the grysbok found in the south-western Cape, but is slightly smaller and lacks the 'false hoofs' which are present on the hindlegs of the latter.

Although it occurs widely through the Kruger National Park, its distribution pattern is somewhat patchy, and it is certainly more common in the eastern half than in the west. It appears to prefer broken or hilly country with low-growing scrub and low grass, and it shuns woodland and stands of long grass. Visitors to the Park occasionally confuse Sharpe's grysbok with the steenbok, but there are several distinguishing features. The steenbok carries its head high even when it is running. It has obvious white underparts and its vertically set horns are six- to 10 centimetres long; Sharpe's grysbok, on the other hand, holds its head low, has buffy underparts and has five-centimetre-long, backward-sloping horns. In addition, the rich reddish-brown coat of Sharpe's grysbok is liberally sprinkled with white hairs, giving its pelage a distinctly grizzled appearance.

As yet, no in-depth study has been carried out into the social structure and habits of this shy little antelope. It is likely, however, to be similar to the steenbok, occurring solitarily, in pairs, or as a small family group of ewe, ram and lamb. It is more nocturnal than the steenbok, although can be seen browsing and grazing in the late afternoon or early morning.

SPOTTED HYAENA

SPOTTED HYAENA
Crocuta crocuta
GEVLEKTE HIËNA

The spotted hyaena is the larger of the two hyaena species of southern Africa – and the more successful. Its rare cousin the brown hyaena, although certainly resident in the Park in the 1920s and 1930s, is now hardly ever seen. The spotted hyaena, on the other hand, is relatively common throughout the Park, being particularly abundant in the central districts.

It has an ungainly appearance, with heavy forequarters sloping down to slender hindquarters. The large, blunt-nosed head is equipped with an exceptionally robust set of teeth and very strongly developed temporal and masseter muscles which together give the spotted hyaena reputedly the most powerful jaws of any living mammal. Male

hyaenas stand about 80 centimetres at the shoulder and have a mass of up to 70 kilograms; the females are slightly taller and on average six or seven kilograms heavier.

The spotted hyaena's social organization is based on a matriarchal system of clans. Although in East Africa a clan may have up to 80 members, in the Kruger National Park it will normally consist of eight to 12 individuals, each clan having a scent-marked home range of about 25 square kilometres. Healthy populations exist in the Park, particularly in the open savanna plains of the central districts.

Hyaenas are primarily nocturnal and although they are opportunistic scavengers they can also be active predators of animals as large as zebra. They forage alone or in small groups, but all clan members will congregate at large carcasses as well as at the communal dens.

BLACK-BACKED JACKALS

BLACK-BACKED JACKAL
Canis mesomelas
ROOIJAKKALS

Standing approximately 40 centimetres at the shoulder, with males weighing about eight kilograms and females about seven kilograms, this handsome member of the dog family can be recognized by the dark blackish saddle on its back (from the nape of its neck to the base of its tail), its reddish flanks and limbs, and its black bushy tail. It is a wary and cunning creature.

The black-backed jackal is distributed throughout the Kruger National Park, but tends to occur in larger numbers in parts of the central districts. It prefers open country where some scrub cover is available. Although nocturnal in farming areas, it can often be seen moving during the day in the Park, either alone or in pairs and occasion-ally in larger parties. It can be quite vocal, especially during the mating season which occurs in late winter, and its 'yaah-ha-ha-ha' call is one of the characteristic sounds of the veld at night.

Carrion is the main component of its diet, but it also hunts actively, preying on small rodents, ground-nesting birds, lizards, dung-beetles, locusts and solifuges.

Two to five (rarely up to nine) pups are born in burrows or rock crevices during spring and summer after a gestation period of 60 to 70 days. Unlike most mammals, black-backed jackals form long-term pair-bonds between dog and bitch and both take part in rearing the offspring. Pups of the previous year's litter may remain with the parents and help to raise the next litter. There appears to be a positive correlation between the number of helpers and the number of young successfully reared.

WILD DOGS

WILD DOG

Lycaon pictus

WILDEHOND

'Give a dog a bad name' is a saying which truly applies to the wild dog of the African plains. Early writers condemned its 'murderous' depredations on game in such strong terms that even today some people hold an unwarranted prejudice against this extremely interesting member of the dog family. No-one will argue with the fact that it is undeniably a very effective, determined and efficient hunter – but it is no more 'murderous' than a cheetah, a lion or any other carnivore.

In certain respects the wild dog differs from the 'true' dogs: it is, for example, exclusively flesh-eating while other dogs eat significant quantities of insects and plant material, and it has only four toes on each forefoot whereas 'true' dogs have five. Its coat coloration is distinctive, consisting of an irregular pattern of black, white and sandy-yellow blotches, and it may also be recognized by its large rounded ears and its bushy white-tipped tail. A male may attain a shoulder height of 75 centimetres and a mass of about 25 kilograms.

Although widespread in the Park, they are mostly seen in the southern district, in the savanna and woodland regions of Skukuza, Pretoriuskop and Malelane; they are also, however, encountered regularly in the Kingfisherspruit Section.

Their usual prey in the Park consists of small- to medium-sized antelope, with impala at the top of the list, although they can kill larger species such as zebra and wildebeest. Chases may continue for up to five kilometres at speeds of between 48 and 60 kilometres an hour.

CHEETAHS

CHEETAH

Acinonyx jubatus

JAGLUIPERD

The lithe, sleek and lovely cheetah is unfortunately not particularly common in the Kruger National Park, the most recent estimate giving a total of 250 animals. Although it is widely distributed in the Park, it is certainly more common in the open woodland, savanna and plains of the southern and central districts.

The cheetah is often confused with the leopard, but the two can easily be distinguished by their spots. The cheetah has 'solid', slightly oval, jet-black spots whereas the leopard has rosette-like spots each of which is made up of a circular cluster of two to five small black blotches. Only the cheetah has the characteristic black 'tear-stripe' curving downwards from the eye to the corner of the mouth. Cheetahs are slightly taller than leopards, standing about 80 centimetres at the shoulder; an average male will attain a mass of approximately 55 kilograms.

It is well known to be the world's fastest land mammal, achieving average sprint speeds of up to 75 kilometres per hour over distances of between 100 and 150 metres; during short bursts, however, it is said to be capable of about 100 kilometres per hour.

With such formidable running powers, the cheetah should be a very successful hunter; in fact, it lacks stamina, and if the prey animal is not overtaken within a short distance, the cheetah will abandon the chase. Even after a successful hunt the unaggressive cheetah may forfeit its prey to more dominant predators such as the lion or hyaena. Small- to medium-sized antelope such as impala constitute its principal prey.

LIONESS WITH CUBS

LION

Panthera leo

LEEU

The lion is the largest African carnivore, males standing up to 125 centimetres at the shoulder and having a mass of as much as 240 kilograms, although rarely more. The heaviest wild lion on record, however, was a 313-kilogram man-eater shot near Hectorspruit just outside the southern border of the Park in 1936. Lionesses are smaller and lighter than their mates, weighing between 110 and 150 kilograms.

Only the males possess the distinctive heavy mane of long hair which serves as a sexual signal to females and also protects the lion's head and neck from the raking claws of rivals during combat. Both male and female lions are very vocal and a fully developed roar can carry for as much as eight kilometres on a quiet night. Roaring often occurs just before dawn and is used to advertise the ownership of a territory. Lions are predominantly nocturnal, but are frequently observed moving or hunting during daylight hours. During the heat of the day, however, they rest in the shade.

The social grouping of lions is the pride, which can be large or small, but in the Park averages between 11 and 12 individuals. A pride may include several males but one will be dominant over the others. Lions prey on a wide variety of large mammals and often hunt in groups to kill species such as giraffe and buffalo. Lionesses do most of the hunting, although the male often appropriates most of the food. In order of preference, their principal prey consists of wildebeest, impala, zebra, waterbuck and kudu. There are some 2 000 lions widely distributed throughout the Park.

LEOPARD

LEOPARD
Panthera pardus
LUIPERD

The leopard is the largest of the African spotted cats (although the cheetah is slightly taller) and is a powerful nocturnal predator. It has a wide habitat tolerance and is common and widespread through the Park, especially in dense riverine vegetation and in rocky hills or koppies. The males are larger than the females, standing 60 to 70 centimetres at the shoulder and having a mass of around 60 kilograms.

Unlike the cheetah's spots which are solid black ovals or circles, the leopard's spots are only solid on the head, limbs and underparts; over the back and sides the 'spots' are in fact rosettes made up of two to five small black blotches. No two leopards have identical spot patterns – a fact which permits them to be individually identified by researchers.

They are not often seen, being solitary, secretive and mainly nocturnal creatures. Their night vision is acute, indeed their senses of sight, smell and hearing are all exceptionally well developed. A wide variety of prey items is taken, from insects, fish, reptiles and birds, to mammals ranging in size from mice to kudu. In the Park, however, impala make up about 80 per cent of the leopard's diet. A large prey item is often dragged up a tree for safe storage. Although not normally aggressive towards man, a leopard that is cornered or wounded can be extremely dangerous.

Males hold and defend territories which are shared by females, and both sexes mark their ranges by spraying urine. The litter of between one and three cubs is born after a gestation period of about 100 days.

PHOTO ACCESS/LEX HES

LEOPARD

CARACAL

CARACAL
Felis caracal
ROOIKAT

The caracal is a graceful, medium-sized, long-legged cat, recognizable by its uniform reddish-tan coat which is usually grizzled with silvery-white hairs, its short tail and its long tufted ears. It is a powerful and robust predator, with males standing approximately 40 centimetres at the shoulder and with a mass of about 17 kilograms. In the Kruger National Park it is widespread, but tends to be associated with woodland savanna and broken country where it can find cover in stands of tall grass and scrub.

Caracals are not normally encountered during the day when they lie up in thick bush or grass, and are most active at dusk and during the night, when they prey on a wide variety of animals, from reptiles and ground-nesting birds to monkeys, dassies, mice and the young of larger antelope such as bushbuck, impala and reedbuck. Caracals will occasionally attack prey heavier than themselves. They are adept tree-climbers. In certain areas of South Africa the 'rooikat' is detested by farmers as a killer of small stock such as sheep and goats and is hunted mercilessly.

The caracal's secretive and nocturnal ways have discouraged detailed studies of its biology in the field. It is, however, known to be a solitary animal, associating in pairs for mating purposes only. The female produces her litter of two to three kittens in a disused aardvark burrow or in a hole in the bole of a large tree, after a gestation period of just over two months. The kittens become independent when they are nine to 12 months old. In the Park it seems that kittens are born in July and August.

SERVAL

SERVAL
Felis serval
TIERBOSKAT

This handsome spotted cat is the rarest of the three smaller cat species in the Kruger National Park. It has a tawny-yellow coat beautifully marked with black spots, blotches and bars, and to some it may appear somewhat like a smaller version of the cheetah. Its elegant appearance is enhanced by its long legs, graceful neck and conspicuous large ears. Full-grown males attain a mass of around 11 kilograms, the females slightly less. It is a medium-sized cat with a shoulder height of about 60 centimetres to the cheetah's 80 centimetres. Its relatively short tail also distinguishes it from the cheetah; about 30 centimetres long it only reaches half-way to the ground – the cheetah's can reach the ground.

Although not common, the serval is widespread through the Kruger National Park, associated particularly with grassland savannas such as the tall grassveld areas in the Pretoriuskop Section and the palm-studded plains of the northern Lebombo Flats. Proximity to water appears to be an essential habitat requirement and it has a liking for the undergrowth near rivers and spruits. One to three kittens are born during the summer.

Its long legs allow fast movement over short distances and it has incredible leaping powers which are used to good effect pursuing prey through long grass. It is also an expert climber and will seek refuge from its enemies in trees. By day, the serval conceals itself in long grass, reeds or under bushes; at night it emerges to hunt, taking mostly rodents, birds (such as weavers and guinea-fowl) and other small creatures.

AFRICAN WILDCAT

AFRICAN WILDCAT

Felis lybica

VAALBOSKAT

The African wildcat looks very much like the domestic cat, which is perhaps not too surprising as it was from North African wildcat stock that the ancient Egyptians domesticated the tabby some 5 000 years ago. Their close relationship means that wild- and domestic cats can interbreed freely wherever their ranges overlap and there is a real danger that the African wildcat will be hybridized out of existence in some areas. To prevent this happening in the Kruger National Park, domestic cats are not allowed as staff pets unless they have been neutered.

The true wildcat can be distinguished from the domestic cat by its longer legs with transverse black bands, its proportionately shorter tail and the reddish sheen over its belly and behind its ears. It is abundant in the Park – the most common of the three small cat species – with a wide habitat tolerance although it prefers lightly-wooded country or long-grass areas.

Although it is primarily nocturnal, the wildcat can be active on overcast days. It is a solitary, secretive hunter, predominantly preying on rodents, but also taking hares, reptiles, birds, spiders and insects as well as wild fruit. It is very adept at climbing trees. The species is very territorial and both sexes scent-mark (with urine) and defend the territory.

Two to five kittens are born during the summer, after a gestation period of some 60 to 65 days, and are hidden in holes in the ground dug by other species such as aardvark or spring-hare, in rock crevices or in dense undergrowth.

PHOTO ACCESS/J&B PHOTOGRAPHERS

PHOTO ACCESS/G.P.J.DU P.ESSIS

CIVET

CIVET
Civettictis civetta
SIWET

The civet, which is often incorrectly called the 'civet-cat', is the largest South African representative of the mongoose family, the Viverridae. It is a distinctive animal, with its long body boldly marked with an attractive pattern of black, grey and white blotches and stripes. Its fur is long and coarse, especially in the dorsal crest along the spine from forehead to tail-tip; this crest is erected during threat-displays. Female civets are slightly heavier than males, both having a mass of about 11 kilograms and standing about 38 centimetres at the arched contour of the back.

Civets usually prefer to live in well-watered areas where sufficient cover is available in the form of high grass or palm thickets. Although they are mainly nocturnal in habit they are occasionally seen abroad in the early morning or on overcast days. They take a wide range of food items from millipedes, insects, rodents and birds, to reptiles, amphibians and even fish – the latter taken under water. Carrion is also a major food resource. Fruit, however, is another important constituent of the civet's diet, marula and buffalo-thorn berries being two noteworthy examples.

The civet is solitary by nature and tends to use paths and roads in its nocturnal wanderings, characteristically moving along with its head held low. It deposits its faeces at communal 'latrines' known as civetries. Smooth-surfaced objects along its line of march are scent-marked with the secretion of the perineal glands under the tail; this secretion, known as 'civet', was formerly used in the manufacture of perfumes.

SMALL-SPOTTED GENET   LARGE-SPOTTED GENET

SMALL-SPOTTED GENET
Genetta genetta
KLEINKOLMUSKEJAATKAT

LARGE-SPOTTED GENET
Genetta tigrina
GROOTKOLMUSKEJAATKAT

Both South African genet species occur in the Kruger National Park and as they are similar in appearance and habits it is useful to describe them together.

Genets are slender-bodied, short-legged and graceful little carnivores with a light-brown pelage attractively marked with rusty-brown, dark-brown or black spots and bars. As their names imply, the small-spotted genet usually has smaller spots than the large-spotted genet, but this is not always the case. A better field character is the colour of the tip of the tail – white in the small-spotted genet, black in the large-spotted genet. The tails of both species are ringed in alternate bands of black (or brown) and white hair, approximately eight of each. Both species have a black or dark-brown stripe down the middle of the back, but in the case of the small-spotted genet this is associated with a band of long hair along the spine which can be erected into a high-standing crest when the animal is under stress. Body mass in both genets is in the order of 1,5 to 2,0 kilograms.

Although both genets are found virtually throughout the Park, the small-spotted genet is more common in the southern half and the large-spotted genet is more common in the north. The two species are both savanna inhabitants but the large-spotted genet is more strictly associated with well-watered areas while the small-spotted genet can tolerate more arid conditions and is independent of surface water. Like other genet species, both South African forms are generally solitary in habit, nocturnal and terrestrial although partly arboreal. The diet of both consists of rats, mice, birds, snakes, lizards, frogs, insects, scorpions and fruit.

PHOTO ACCESS/LEX HES

WHITE-TAILED MONGOOSE

WHITE-TAILED MONGOOSE

Ichneumia albicauda

WITSTERTMUISHOND

The white-tailed mongoose is the largest of the 11 mongoose species of South Africa and is widely distributed throughout the Kruger National Park, especially south of the Olifants River. It favours savanna and grassland habitats where surface water is available. Adult males have a mass of about 4,5 kilograms and measure just over a metre in length from nose to tail-tip (although lengths of one and a half metres have been recorded). The tail is long – about 40 per cent of the total length – and is white for four-fifths of its length from the tip. (Selous's mongoose, which also occurs in the Park, although very rare, is smaller and only one-third of its tail from the tip is white.) The overall colour of the white-

tailed mongoose is grey which is tinged with dark brown, and the legs and feet are pitch-black.

White-tailed mongooses are nocturnal and solitary in habit. They lie up during the day in holes and among thick bushes and emerge at sundown to hunt. Although they are accomplished diggers when in search of earthworms and insect larvae, they do not appear to dig their own burrows, seemingly preferring deserted aardvark or spring-hare holes. Two or three young are born in each litter in burrows such as these during the summer months.

They walk with a fast, restless gait, with head and tail carried low. Frogs and toads feature prominently in their diet and they are known to be good swimmers. Insects, however, appear to comprise the bulk of their diet, followed by amphibians, rodents, reptiles and earthworms.

BANDED MONGOOSES

BANDED MONGOOSE
Mungos mungo
GEBANDE MUISHOND

The banded mongoose is easily recognized by its series – usually 12 to 15 – of black transverse stripes on its back, from behind the shoulder to the base of the tail. It is a small mongoose, measuring around 58 centimetres from nose to tail-tip (the tail is about 40 per cent of this length) and it can attain a mass of 1,3 kilograms. Its coat is somewhat coarse and wiry, the individual hairs having alternating annulations or bands of black, white and brown which give the banded mongoose a somewhat grizzled appearance.

Like the dwarf mongoose, the banded mongoose is a gregarious species, occurring in packs of between five and 60 individuals. Active in the day-time, it spends the night in the shelter of old termite-mounds, piles of boulders or similar refuges, which are an essential component of the banded mongoose's habitat as they are vulnerable to predation by birds of prey.

It may be seen throughout the Park in a variety of savanna, scrub or thicket habitats. Hunting is undertaken communally, the troop members chattering incessantly as they go. They follow each other so closely that the visual effect from a distance is that of a large snake winding its way through the vegetation. They are inquisitive and often stand up on their hindfeet to scan their immediate environment. Their favourite foods include scorpions, beetles, solifuges, birds' eggs, rodents and fruit. Between two and eight young are born during summer in grass-lined chambers in their warrens after a gestation period of approximately two months.

DWARF MONGOOSES

DWARF MONGOOSE
Helogale parvula
DWERGMUISHOND

The intriguing little dwarf mongoose is the smallest of the 11 mongoose species which occur in South Africa. It is a common species throughout the Kruger National Park, occurring in savanna environments particularly in the western parts. An adult can attain a mass of about a third of a kilogram (compared with that of the banded mongoose at up to 1,5 kilograms) and males and females are the same size. At a distance the dwarf mongoose appears black or very dark brown but at close range the coat has a 'pepper-and-salt' grizzled appearance with flecks of white or buff.

Dwarf mongooses, like the banded mongooses, are gregarious by nature and associate in troops of 20 or more individuals.

They are active during the day and at night lie up in old termite-mounds or in warrens in rocky areas which they excavate themselves. Perhaps the main enemies of dwarf mongooses are birds of prey, consequently they have to be cautious in the open and require ready access to familiar emergency refuges such as dead trees and hollow logs scattered at strategic intervals throughout their home range.

They are inquisitive and bold and will often sit up on their haunches or stand on their hindlegs to assess the situation in their immediate environs. While foraging, troop members maintain vocal contact with sharp chirruping calls. Their prey consists of insects, centipedes, spiders, small reptiles and rodents. Like other mongoose species they will tackle and kill poisonous snakes, with a fascinating combination of daring and caution.

HONEY-BADGER

HONEY-BADGER
Mellivora capensis
RATEL

The stockily built honey-badger is well represented in the Kruger National Park and occurs in practically all habitat types although it does tend to avoid forested areas. As its name suggests, this powerful carnivore has a special fondness for honey and can be extremely destructive of commercial apiaries, often completely wrecking the beehive in its efforts to gain access to the honeycomb.

The honey-badger is unmistakable in the field. Its distinctive coat colour – jet-black below contrasting with the pure white or grey-brown 'saddle' above – is an excellent example of warning coloration. It has a well-deserved reputation as a formidable and fearless fighter, and brooks interference from neither man nor beast (nor man's vehicles). Its weapons are the powerful knife-like claws on its forefeet, and its robust jaws and teeth. Defences are provided by its unusually tough hide which not only protects it from bee-stings but is also so loosely attached to the underlying tissues – it was once described as 'hanging like a loose coating of rubber' – that it is difficult for an attacker to gain a grip. In addition, when the animal is under stress its anal glands discharge a foul-smelling exudate.

Although sometimes active by day, the honey-badger is essentially nocturnal. It lives singly or in pairs and produces a litter of two in a burrow. Both sexes are of similar size with a mass of around 12 kilograms and a shoulder height of approximately 26 centimetres. The diet includes reptiles, rodents, birds, insects and – of course – bee larvae and honey.

CAPE CLAWLESS OTTER

CAPE CLAWLESS OTTER

Aonyx capensis

GROOTOTTER

Of South Africa's two otter species, only the Cape clawless otter occurs in the Kruger National Park. It is relatively common in all of the Park's perennial rivers and may also be found in swamps, dams and permanent pools in seasonal rivers. Although this otter can on occasion be found some distance away from water, presumably when searching for different feeding-grounds, fresh water is an essential habitat requirement for the Cape clawless otter. Access to sources of fresh water is also a necessary habitat requirement for those otters which live in estuarine and coastal waters.

The Cape clawless otter is long-bodied, sleek-furred and short-legged, dark brown above with a distinctive white throat and upper breast. It can attain a mass of up to 18 kilograms. Its muscular tail, thickened at the base and flattened underneath, is used for propulsion under water; the toes of the hindfeet are webbed for half their length and also assist in swimming. There are no claws on the forefeet and only rudimentary nails are present on the hindfeet, on the third and fourth toes. The undersides of the digits are rough to assist the otter in holding slippery prey.

Although fish, small leguaans, insects, mammals and birds are preyed upon by Cape clawless otters, they appear to favour crabs and frogs. Their faeces are deposited near the water's edge and contain the indigestible remains of their prey – fragments of crabs and molluscs, fish-scales and bones. Cape clawless otters are diurnal and nocturnal and are found alone, in pairs, or in small family parties.

43

THICK-TAILED BUSHBABY

LESSER BUSHBABY

THICK-TAILED BUSHBABY
Otolemur crassicaudatus
BOSNAGAAP

LESSER BUSHBABY
Galago moholi
NAGAPIE

These interesting and attractive primates may be encountered in well-wooded areas throughout the Park, although the lesser bushbaby is the more widespread, being primarily associated with acacia woodland savanna, although it is also found in mopane savanna in the north of the Park. The thick-tailed bushbaby is associated with riverine forests, thickets and more well-developed woodlands. They may, on occasion, share the same habitats.

Bushbabies are vocal animals and can utter a wide variety of calls, some of which are plaintive-sounding and resemble those of a crying baby. The name 'bushbaby' may be derived from these cries but perhaps also from the animal's cute and cuddly-looking appearance – its soft woolly coat and long furry tail, its large eyes and mobile ears.

The thick-tailed bushbaby is considerably larger than the lesser bushbaby with a mass of around 1,2 kilograms to the lesser bushbaby's 150 grams. Bushbabies are extremely agile leapers, the lesser bushbaby being credited with single leaps of up to seven metres. The feet are suitably adapted for grasping branches and the tail is used for balance. Their leaps are frog-like, and on the ground lesser bushbabies hop on their hindlegs like diminutive kangaroos.

The large eyes of bushbabies give them excellent night vision; they shine with a reddish glow if caught in the beam of a torch or car headlights. Both species feed extensively on the gums and resins which exude from the branches of various trees such as acacias, but they also feed on fruit, berries, insects, birds' eggs and, particularly in the case of the thick-tailed bushbaby, on small vertebrates such as birds and reptiles.

CHACMA BABOON: FEMALE WITH BABY

CHACMA BABOON

Papio ursinus

KAAPSE BOBBEJAAN

The chacma baboon is a common species throughout the Kruger National Park and needs little introduction. It is an active, noisy, gregarious and prominent inhabitant of both savanna and montane areas, also occurring marginally on open grassland. Male baboons are markedly larger and heavier than females, with a mass of between 27 and 44 kilograms; females weigh between 14 and 18 kilograms. They carry their tails in a characteristic posture, with the first portion held upwards and the rest drooping downwards, as if broken one-third of the way along.

Although they are mainly terrestrial in habit, they are excellent climbers and utilize either tall trees or ledges on cliff-faces as sleeping-sites and night-time refuges.

Baboons are omnivorous, although largely vegetarian. Their diet consists of fruit, leaves, grasses, bulbs, tubers and flowers as well as insects, scorpions, lizards, birds' eggs, birds and even the new-born young of antelope. Cannibalism has been recorded on occasion, the males eating the young of displaced or deceased males. Permanent water is an essential habitat requirement.

The average baboon troop in the Park consists of 30 to 40 individuals, although troops have been recorded with as many as 100 members. Larger troops may contain several dominant, high-ranking males who share in the troop's offensive and defensive actions and who are the most successful in mating activities. When danger threatens, the subordinate animals – females and young – cluster in the centre of the group, protected by the dominant males, with other males surrounding this nucleus in front, behind and along the flanks.

Baboons are difficult to census, but in 1985 scientists counted 128 troops in the Kruger National Park south of Punda Maria – clearly a healthy state of affairs.

VERVET MONKEY FAMILY

VERVET MONKEY
Cercopithecus aethiops
BLOUAAP

Vervet monkeys are common residents of the Kruger National Park, occurring widespread in savanna woodland but showing a distinct preference for river-bank vegetation and wooded areas near water. They have grizzled, greyish coats, black faces framed in white, black hands and feet and whitish underparts. Monkeys living along the Crocodile River in the Malelane area have a rufous-coloured mane and tail. Adult males are characterized by their bright turquoise or cobalt-blue genitalia. Males are heavier than females, weighing between four and eight kilograms; females weigh between three and five kilograms.

The vervet monkey is widely distributed through East, Central and southern Africa.

It is as much at home on the ground as in trees and is able to exploit a wide variety of habitat types. Primarily vegetarian, it also takes insects, birds and their eggs, scorpions and other small animals as well as fruit, berries, leaves, shoots, roots and bulbs.

Vervet monkeys are preyed upon by leopards, pythons and the larger eagles such as the crowned eagle, but when a predator is spotted during the day the monkeys set up a raucous chattering, follow it and betray its movements to the wildlife community at large. They live in troops of up to 20 individuals, each troop having a well-defined home range. At night they sleep either in rocky shelters or in the canopy of large trees, in small groups of two or three for warmth and companionship. There is a clear order of dominance within troops, but their social relationships are not as rigid as they are in baboon society.

46

PANGOLIN

PANGOLIN

Manis temminckii

IETERMAGOG

Pangolins are solitary, nocturnal animals – although they may be seen during the early morning – and are found throughout the Park especially where termite-mounds are abundant. Although they have a wide habitat tolerance, they do not occur in forests, preferring savannas and woodlands.

The pangolin is one of the most unusual mammals to be found in the Kruger National Park. This quaint and unmistakable creature has been endowed by Nature with a suit of armour in the form of tough brown overlapping scales composed of modified agglutinated hair. These scales cover the pangolin's entire body surface except for the underparts and the sides of the face. When the threat of danger arises, the pangolin rolls itself into a tight ball with its head inside and with the scales of the back and tail protecting its vulnerable parts. As an additional defence measure it can secrete a foul-smelling substance from its anal glands.

The hindlegs of the pangolin are better developed than the forelegs and although it can walk normally on all fours, it tends to walk on the hindfeet only, keeping the forelegs and tail clear of the ground. Pangolins often stand up on their hindlegs in order to look around. Each forefoot is equipped with strong claws with which it digs into ants' nests in search of its prey. Although it feeds primarily on formicid ants, it also eats certain species of termites which it gathers up with its extremely long tongue. As it has no teeth, the ants and termites are ground up by the muscular stomach, aided by ingested grit.

PORCUPINE

TREE-SQUIRREL

PORCUPINE

Hystrix africaeaustralis
YSTERVARK

Porcupines are stout, heavily built animals with blunt, rounded heads, beady, pig-like eyes and an unmistakable coat of long black-and-white quills. The quills cover the porcupine's back and flanks from shoulder to tail and are stout, strong, sharply pointed weapons of defence up to 30 centimetres in length. A crest of long, pliable spines up to 50 centimetres in length extends from the top of the head to the shoulders.

When the animal is annoyed or attacked it raises the crest and quills and presents a formidable barrier to the potential predator. It may also run backwards at a predator which may be injured by the quills, as they tend to come loose from the porcupine and embed themselves in the would-be attacker.

The porcupine is the largest rodent in Africa, with males attaining an average mass of 17 kilograms and females 18,5 kilograms. It is a nocturnal creature, travelling alone, in pairs or in small family groups and feeding on bulbs, tubers, roots, fruit, bark and sometimes carrion. In the Kruger National Park it is common and occurs in most habitat types.

TREE-SQUIRREL

Paraxerus cepapi
BOOMEEKHORING

The tree-squirrel is the most common and widely distributed of the four species of arboreal squirrel in southern Africa, as well as one of the most common and widespread of all the mammal species of the Kruger National Park. Its preferred habitats are savanna woodland and dry forest, but it avoids dense forest. Although frequently found in trees along watercourses, it does not appear to be dependent on surface water. Particularly common in mopane woodland, it is sometimes called the 'mopane squirrel'.

Its coat colour varies widely over its range but in the Park tends to be buffy with a rufous tinge to the upper parts of the limbs. Albinism has been recorded, particularly in the area north of the Olifants River.

Tree-squirrels are active only by day and spend the night in nests in holes in trees, either natural or those made by barbets or woodpeckers. They subsist on berries, seeds, pods, flowers, forbs and grasses, and on insects at certain times of the year. Breeding occurs throughout the year with one to three young per litter.

SCRUB-HARE

ROCK-DASSIES

SCRUB-HARE
Lepus saxatilis
KOLHAAS

The scrub-hare is the most common of the three hare species of the Transvaal Lowveld and is also the largest, attaining a mass of between two and three kilograms. It has conspicuously large ears and a prominent white spot on the forehead from which its Afrikaans common name, *kolhaas*, is derived (*kol*: spot). The soft woolly coat is greyish above, speckled with black, and pure white below. The tail is jet-black above and pure white below, the white underside being used as a warning flash when the hare flees.

It occurs throughout the Kruger National Park. It has a wide habitat tolerance, although usually associated with savannas (including mopane savanna) and grasslands with tall grass, bushes and scrub, but it is absent from mountainous areas. During the day it lies up in 'forms' – shallow depressions of flattened grass in thick vegetation – and at night it emerges to feed on leaves, stems and rhizomes of various grasses.

Scrub-hares are often caught in the beam of car headlights at night as they feed on the short green grass on roadside verges.

ROCK-DASSIE
Procavia capensis
KLIPDAS

The rock-dassie is a small dark-brown creature with short ears, short sturdy legs and no external tail. In the centre of its back is a patch of long hair overlying a dorsal gland. The hair around the gland is erected during displays of aggression and the gland is believed to play a role in social interaction within their rock shelters.

Dassies require a rocky habitat providing crevices and crannies for shelter. Although they are common in the boulder-strewn koppies between the Olifants and Bububu rivers in the northern part of the Park, they are absent from similar habitat south of the Olifants River. There is, however, a small relict population in the Ntlokweni/Maqili area south of Pretoriuskop.

They are gregarious creatures, active only by day and vegetarian in diet. In spite of their acute senses of hearing and sight they frequently fall prey to such predators as black eagles, leopards and pythons. They are agile rock-climbers and their feet are equipped with specialized pads of glandular tissue which keep the soles permanently moist to permit cohesion to rock surfaces.

WAHLBERG'S EPAULETTED FRUIT-BAT

EGYPTIAN SLIT-FACED BAT

WAHLBERG'S EPAULETTED FRUIT-BAT
Epomophorus wahlbergi
WAHLBERG-WITKOLVRUGTEVLERMUIS

Bats are divided into the megachiropterans or fruit-bats ('flying foxes') and the microchiropterans or insectivorous bats. This division is not as clear-cut as it may seem as some fruit-bats are partly insectivorous, and some 'insectivorous' bats eat fruit. Nevertheless, fruit-bats tend to have large eyes and rely on sight rather than echolocation to find their way about.

This species has been recorded from Pretoriuskop and Malelane in the south and from Punda Maria and Pafuri in the north. Colonies roost in thick foliage of trees, especially along rivers. About 15 centimetres in length, it feeds on fruit such as wild figs and perhaps occasionally on insects.

EGYPTIAN SLIT-FACED BAT
Nycteris thebaica
EGIPTIESE SPLEETNEUSVLERMUIS

As their name suggests, slit-faced bats have a distinctive facial slit from the nostrils to above the eyes. This slit overlies a concave area in the skull which encloses a complex array of nose-leaves, used in echolocation. The nose-leaves are only visible when the slit is open, unlike those of the horseshoe-bats. Slit-faced bats have disproportionately large ears.

The more widespread and common of the two slit-faced bat species in the Park is the Egyptian slit-faced bat, whose ears may be up to 37 millimetres in length compared with a head-and-body length (excluding the tail) of around 55 millimetres. This insectivorous species roosts in caves, under eaves or in hollow tree-trunks by day.

SUNDEVALL'S LEAF-NOSED BAT

SUNDEVALL'S LEAF-NOSED BAT

Hipposideros caffer

SUNDEVALL BLADNEUSVLERMUIS

Sundevall's leaf-nosed bat is a small bat with a total length (including the tail) of about eight centimetres. Insectivorous, it prefers small, soft-bodied insects.

It takes its name from the curious – some may say grotesque – fleshy appendages around its nostrils, known as 'nose-leaves'. These are vitally important for the bat's echolocation system whereby it can detect objects in pitch-darkness by means of reflected sound. Sound impulses are emitted through the nostrils and then channelled and directed by the nose-leaves to a point of focus ahead of the flying bat. Returning echoes from potential obstacles or insect prey are picked up by the bat's ultrasensitive ears, interpreted by its brain and appropriate action is taken, all in a matter of milliseconds.

Several different colour forms occur in Sundevall's leaf-nosed bat, from rich golden-yellow to dark grey-brown and all shades in between. The females have two functional nipples on the breast and a pair of 'false nipples' on the lower abdomen near the base of the tail; these are used by the single offspring as alternative clinging points when it is being transported by its mother during infancy.

It is a gregarious species which lives in colonies of hundreds. The roosts are in caves, rock crevices or under the roofs of buildings. One particular community in a cave at Munywini is known to have lived there continuously for over 20 years. Although widespread in the Park, it favours drier, more open savanna as long as water is readily available.

OSTRICH

DARTER

OSTRICH
Struthio camelus
VOLSTRUIS

The ostrich is the largest living bird, with males up to two metres in height and attaining an average mass of 70 kilograms.

Male ostriches are polygamous, breeding units being one male to three females on average. The hens lay their eggs in one family nest-scrape in sandy soil, each hen laying between three and eight eggs, communal clutches averaging between 16 and 23 eggs. The male usually incubates the eggs at night, the dominant female by day.

Ostriches are conspicuous enough to allow censusing; there are approximately 640 birds in the Kruger National Park, mostly to the north of the Sabie River. They prefer open, flatter areas, shunning hilly country, wooded regions and dense bush.

DARTER
Anhinga melanogaster
SLANGHALSVOËL

Darters are large birds with long necks, somewhat cormorant-like in appearance. Darters may be easily distinguished from cormorants, however, by their bills which are longer, more slender and are sharply pointed. The pronounced kink at the base of the long neck is a characteristic feature and there is a special hinge mechanism at the base of the 8th cervical (neck) vertebra which enables the bird to dart its head and neck rapidly forward to spear fish.

The darters swims low in the water, with only the head and neck showing. In this posture it resembles a water-snake progressing through the water.

They can be found at quiet rivers and dams throughout the Kruger National Park.

GREY HERON

GOLIATH HERON

GREY HERON
Ardea cinerea
BLOUREIER

The grey heron is one of the larger herons, standing about 90 centimetres in height. Males are slightly heavier than females and may attain a mass of two kilograms. It flies slowly and heavily with its feet trailing beyond its tail and with its neck drawn back in an S-shaped curve.

The prey of the grey heron consists of small fish, frogs, crabs, insects, small birds and mammals. The heron normally stands motionless at the water's edge for extended periods, waiting for its potential prey to come within striking distance. Its bill is employed as a grasping instrument and not as a spear.

It occurs throughout the Park at dams and shallow river backwaters.

GOLIATH HERON
Ardea goliath
REUSEREIER

The goliath heron is the largest heron in the world – which makes it easy to identify – with a height of around 140 centimetres. It weighs up to 4,3 kilograms. In flight it is ponderous, even more so than the grey heron, with around 98 wing-beats per minute to the grey heron's 142.

It may be seen standing motionless in shallow water for long periods, waiting for its prey to approach. Prey items include small fish, frogs, crabs, and small reptiles and mammals. With its longer legs it can forage and feed in deeper water than most other herons.

Breeding of the goliath heron has been reported in the Park in summer along the Letaba and Luvuvhu rivers.

53

CATTLE EGRET

GREEN-BACKED HERON

CATTLE EGRET
Bubulcus ibis
BOSLUISVOËL

The cattle egret is a small, gregarious, stockily built white heron which occurs throughout the Kruger National Park in open savanna habitats. It is commonly found in small flocks, attendant on grazing animals and feeding on the insects and other prey disturbed by grazing animals' hoofs. Often it can be seen perching on their backs. It usually forages away from water, and in the evening it gathers in large flocks near rivers and dams.

Outside the breeding season, the cattle egret's plumage is white with olive-brown legs and black feet. In the breeding season, the legs change to a dull yellowish-red colour and pinkish-buff plumes appear on the crown, back and breast.

GREEN-BACKED HERON
Butorides striatus
GROENRUGREIER

A small, short-necked heron with a black cap, grey neck, white throat, blackish-green back and bright orange-yellow legs and feet, it is a solitary and skulking inhabitant of densely vegetated rivers, pools and streams. It occurs throughout the Kruger National Park in suitable habitat and, while not often seen, it is probably the most common heron in the area.

It runs effortlessly over branches and reeds and characteristically stands motionless for long periods with head and neck held horizontally or pointing down at an angle. Prey items include fish, frogs, small reptiles, insects, molluscs and other invertebrates, and they are caught by swift strikes of the heron's bill.

HAMERKOP

MARABOU STORK

HAMERKOP

Scopus umbretta

HAMERKOP

An unmistakable resident of the Kruger National Park, the hamerkop is relatively common wherever standing water can be found. It is a medium-sized (430 grams), stout, plain dark-brown bird with long legs, a sturdy bill and a strong crest of long feathers on the back of its large head. The crest and bill together give it its 'hammer-head' appearance.

It is usually seen singly, but also occurs in pairs or groups of four or five individuals, and forages by wading in shallow water, sometimes shuffling its feet to flush prey from the sediment. The hamerkop feeds particularly on platannas ('clawed toads') but also takes crustaceans, fish and insects.

Its huge, untidy, rounded nest of sticks, approximately two metres in diameter and with a one-metre-thick roof, is usually built in a tree.

MARABOU STORK

Leptoptilos crumeniferus

MARABOE

The marabou stork is a large, long-legged bird with a bald head and neck and with a large inflatable air-sac hanging below its throat. There is another smaller air-sac on the hindneck.

These gregarious, lugubrious-looking birds are carrion-feeders, but will also take live prey when the opportunity arises, from insects and frogs to snakes, the young of crocodiles, birds and rodents. In the Kruger National Park they compete with vultures at carcasses and their numbers may be increasing because of the availability of left-overs from culling operations carried out by the Park authorities.

Marabous are summer migrants to the Kruger National Park, although a few remain to breed in winter, usually in May. Their stick-platform nests are constructed in trees or on cliffs.

WHITE STORK

BLACK STORK

WHITE STORK
Ciconia ciconia
WITOOIEVAAR

The white stork is a migrant from Eurasia, arriving in South Africa in late October and departing in March. Its numbers in the Park vary from year to year. It is a handsome, large bird with a long, bright-red bill, black wings, and a white body and tail. Its legs and feet are red, but during hot weather the stork may excrete on them for a cooling effect, in which case they will appear white or pinkish.

They usually occur in large flocks and forage in marshy areas and open grassland for insects, frogs, reptiles, young birds and rodents. Locust plagues attract white storks in enormous numbers. They utilize thermal air-currents efficiently and can soar for long distances, gliding from thermal to thermal.

BLACK STORK
Ciconia nigra
GROOTSWARTOOIEVAAR

The black stork is similar in size to the white stork but is glossy brownish-black on its head, neck, wings, back and uppertail; its belly and undertail are white and its bill and legs are red.

Unlike the white stork, the black stork feeds extensively in water, catching fish, frogs, tadpoles and crabs; however, it will take reptiles, small mammals and nestling birds. It is not normally gregarious and is usually seen singly or in pairs, and sometimes in small groups. Outside the breeding season it may be more gregarious.

It breeds in winter and makes its nest on a cliff-ledge or in a cave. Black storks from the Transvaal Highveld breeding population move to the Lowveld and Park in summer.

ABDIM'S STORK

OPEN-BILLED STORK

ABDIM'S STORK
Ciconia abdimii
KLEINSWARTOOIEVAAR

Abdim's stork is a very gregarious trans-equatorial migrant which breeds north of the Equator in the northern summer and spends the southern summer (October to April) in southern Africa. Its appearance in the Kruger National Park is erratic; some years it may arrive in large numbers and disperse widely, but at other times no birds arrive at all. This fluctuation may be correlated with rainfall or the availability of insects, but is not yet fully understood.

Black in colour except for the white belly, rump and lower back, Abdim's stork eats large insects, frogs, mice and fish which it catches in the open veld and in marshes and pools. Like the white and black storks, it can soar effortlessly.

OPEN-BILLED STORK
Anastomus lamelligerus
OOPBEKOOIEVAAR

The open-billed stork is an unmistakable medium-sized, brownish-black stork with an extraordinary bill whose mandibles meet at the tip but have a wide visible gap in the centre. It feeds exclusively on molluscs, for which prey its bill is specially adapted. The muscles which hold the snail within the shell, or which keep a bivalve's shell closed, are deftly severed by the stork's blade like lower mandible.

In the Kruger National Park it is a resident species but it is only regularly seen at Nwanetsi and Gudzani. It feeds solitarily but is otherwise gregarious. In years of abundant rain it breeds colonially on the flood-pans of the Limpopo River. Breeding may cease for years during long droughts.

SADDLE-BILLED STORK

SADDLE-BILLED STORK
Ephippiorhynchus senegalensis
SAALBEKOOIEVAAR

The saddle-billed stork is the tallest African stork and is quite unmistakable in the field with its huge, slightly upturned red-and-black bill with a distinctive yellow frontal shield or 'saddle'. Its overall plumage is black and white, and the contrasting wing pattern is evident in flight.

It can be seen alone or in pairs, frequenting rivers, pans, swamps and dams, usually in lightly wooded country, where it forages in shallow water, catching fish weighing up to 0,5 kilograms as well as frogs and other small vertebrates in or near the water.

It occurs throughout the Kruger National Park, but in the dry months during winter is found near permanent pools such as those in the Tshokwane, Nwanetsi and Nshawu areas.

PHOTO ACCESS/LEX HES

GERA D CUBITT

HADEDA IBIS

WHITE-FACED DUCKS

HADEDA IBIS
Bostrychia hagedash
HADEDA

The hadeda is a widespread resident species in the Kruger National Park. It is gregarious and usually occurs in flocks of five to 20 birds, preferring habitats near open water, such as those along some of the perennial rivers and around the larger dams. The hadeda roosts in small groups in trees, and its diet includes insects, snails, spiders and earthworms as well as small vertebrates such as lizards.

The call of the hadeda is unmistakable: it is a loud, raucous, harsh-sounding 'haaa' or 'ha-de-daa', emitted at take-off and in flight, and often repeated. Its plumage is a dull greyish-brown and the decurved bill has a red stripe running along the ridge of the upper mandible. The sexes are alike.

WHITE-FACED DUCK
Dendrocygna viduata
NONNETJIE-EEND

The white-faced duck is a nomadic resident species in the Kruger National Park, and has been recorded from various waterbodies throughout the area. It is a gregarious species, but in the Park usually occurs in small flocks of birds which are subject to local movements.

It derives its name from the white coloration of the front half of the head, and is the only duck in the Park with this distinguishing feature. It has an upright posture and a long neck with a chestnut breast and a black belly. Food items include buds, seeds and rhizomes of aquatic plants, but it will also take insect larvae, molluscs and crustaceans; these are obtained by wading, dabbling or up-ending in shallow water.

EGYPTIAN GOOSE

KNOB-BILLED DUCK MALE

ALAN WEAVING

CHRIS AND TILDE STUART

EGYPTIAN GOOSE

Alopochen aegyptiacus

KOLGANS

This large brown-and-white goose with its distinctive brown eye-patch and brown 'inverted horseshoe' patch on its breast is widespread at rivers and dams throughout the Kruger National Park. It is a heavy bird, with the gander having a mass of around 2,5 kilograms and the goose 2,0 kilograms. Its diet is primarily vegetarian, consisting of grass, leaves, seeds and seedlings, and the rhizomes and tubers of aquatic plants.

Breeding probably occurs throughout the year in the Park and nests may be on the ground in dense vegetation or in trees or on cliff-ledges.

Despite its bulk, the Egyptian goose is a fast flier. It is a strong diver, but this skill is usually only utilized during the moult.

KNOB-BILLED DUCK

Sarkidiornis melanotos

KNOBBELEEND

This large duck is sexually dimorphic, that is the sexes are markedly different in appearance. Both are black above and white below, but the male is much larger than the female and has a large, laterally compressed black knob on the top of its bill. This appendage is under hormonal control, and reaches peak size during the breeding season. Outside the breeding season it is reduced in size and may even fall over. Males are sometimes polygynous, having up to three females each.

The knob-billed duck loafs for much of the day on the shores of open waters. It feeds on the seeds of grass and water-lilies but will occasionally take locusts and aquatic insect larvae.

SPUR-WINGED GOOSE

SECRETARY-BIRD

SPUR-WINGED GOOSE
Plectropterus gambensis
WILDEMAKOU

The spur-winged goose is the largest of the southern African waterfowl with males attaining a mass of up to ten kilograms, and females up to 4,5 kilograms. Adults are black above with white underparts but the amount of white on the face, neck, breast and shoulders varies from one individual to the next. The bill, frontal knob, bare facial skin and legs are red. Each wing-shoulder has a sharp spur, which in males is about 20 millimetres long, and is used in fights between rival ganders.

Spur-winged geese are summer visitors to the Park. They occur widespread through the area, singly or in flocks of up to 20 birds, on the sand-banks of rivers, at pans, or even at isolated puddles.

SECRETARY-BIRD
Sagittarius serpentarius
SEKRETARISVOËL

This fascinating and distinctive bird of prey is a fairly common resident throughout the Kruger National Park in open or lightly wooded country. Although it is adapted to a terrestrial way of life – as is evident by its long legs and short toes – it can fly and soar well on its broad and powerful wings. The male stands approximately 130 centimetres in height and may attain a weight of up to four kilograms.

It is usually seen alone or in pairs, striding purposefully through the veld scrutinizing the ground for its prey of insects, lizards, frogs, rodents, birds' eggs and nestlings, and snakes. It is capable of killing large venomous snakes with powerful stamping blows of its feet.

HOODED VULTURE

WHITE-BACKED VULTURE

HOODED VULTURE

Necrosyrtes monachus
MONNIKAASVOËL

The hooded vulture occurs over a large area in the Kruger National Park, favouring open woodland and savanna habitats. It is a medium-sized, dark-brown vulture with a slender bill.

Although it is generally seen singly or in pairs, it does occur in groups of up to nine at a carcass where, however, it cannot compete with the larger vulture species and has to make do with scraps left or dropped by its relatives.

One of the interesting characteristics of the adult hooded vulture is its ability to 'blush'. The bare skin on the sides of the face is normally pink, but flushes bright red when the bird is excited. It may turn greenish-white when the vulture is threatened.

WHITE-BACKED VULTURE

Gyps africanus
WITRUGAASVOËL

The white-backed vulture is a medium-sized vulture with a mass of approximately 5,4 kilograms and a wingspan in the region of 2,2 metres. It is a light tawny-brown colour with a white back and rump by which it can be distinguished from the Cape vulture. The skin on the face and neck is dark grey or blackish, the crop patch is brown and the bill is black.

This gregarious species is a relatively abundant resident of the Kruger National Park and is in fact the most common of the five vultures species occurring there. It feeds deep within a carcass, tearing off flesh with its very effective razor-sharp bill and using its muscular barbed tongue to force the meat down its throat.

LAPPET-FACED VULTURE

CAPE VULTURE

LAPPET-FACED VULTURE
Torgos tracheliotus
SWARTAASVOËL

The lappet-faced vulture is the largest southern African vulture in size, although it weighs slightly less than the Cape vulture. It is a spectacular bird in appearance, with white 'trousers' and breast contrasting with the overall black coloration of the rest of its body. The bare pink head and throat have folds or 'lappets', from which the vulture derives its name.

It is a common resident of the Park but is less gregarious than other vulture species, usually seen singly or in pairs. When it arrives at a carcass, it dominates all other vulture species present, and with its stout bill is quite capable of opening even the carcasses of thick-skinned animals such as the rhinoceros, hippopotamus and elephant.

CAPE VULTURE
Gyps coprotheres
KRANSAASVOËL

This attractive vulture is found only in southern Africa and has suffered an alarming reduction in range and numbers in recent years. Adult birds are almost as large as the lappet-faced vulture and are in fact heavier, with a mass of between eight and 11 kilograms. It is almost white overall with strongly contrasting ash-brown or blackish wings and tail.

The Cape vulture is a highly gregarious species which occurs throughout the Park, but is most common in the south and during the summer. It does not, however, breed in the Park, the nearest colony being 64 kilometres west of Orpen Gate. It is aggressive at carcasses and feeds deep within the body cavity of dead animals.

TAWNY EAGLE

WAHLBERG'S EAGLE

TAWNY EAGLE
Aquila rapax
ROOFAREND

The plumage of the tawny eagle varies from dark brown to pale brown, with occasional individuals having an almost white appearance. Feet are bright yellow. Males and females are alike; both have feathered legs resembling baggy trousers.

The tawny eagle prefers open or lightly wooded country and is a fairly common and widespread resident of the Park. It is versatile in its feeding habits, being a predator, a scavenger and even a pirate as the situation demands. Carrion is an important part of its diet, from small road-kills to antelope; but it can be rapacious, harrying other eagles to steal their food and killing such animals as dassies, mongooses and the young of small antelope.

WAHLBERG'S EAGLE
Aquila wahlbergi
BRUINAREND

This handsome small eagle is a migrant to southern Africa from tropical Africa north of the Equator, arriving here in August and departing in March/April. Like the tawny eagle its plumage shows variable colouring, most individuals being uniform dark brown but with a substantial number of birds being honey-brown, pale brown or almost white. Its legs are fully feathered and the sexes look alike.

Wahlberg's eagle frequents woodland and savanna woodland and may be found in all parts of the Kruger National Park during the summer – at which time it is in fact the most common eagle in the Park. A solitary, unobtrusive species, it feeds on insects, birds, reptiles, and small mammals.

MARTIAL EAGLE

AFRICAN HAWK-EAGLE

MARTIAL EAGLE
Polemaetus bellicosus
BREËKOPAREND

The martial eagle is the largest African eagle Although the sexes look alike, the female is considerably larger than the male and may attain a mass of over six kilograms and a wingspan of up to 2,6 metres. Its long, broad wings enable it to soar high in the sky, sometimes beyond the range of human vision It possesses acute eyesight and can launch an attack on a prey animal from as far as six kilometres away.

Although it is regarded as 'common' and widespread in the Kruger National Park, its large territory requirements – 100 square kilometres per pair – restrict its numbers to an estimated 110 breeding pairs. Prey items include game-birds, waterfowl, reptiles and mammals up to the size of common duikers.

AFRICAN HAWK-EAGLE
Hieraaetus fasciatus
GROOTJAGAREND

The African hawk-eagle is a conspicuous medium-sized bird of prey with blackish upperparts and white underparts which are boldly streaked with black. A true hunting eagle, it surprises its prey from low altitudes, often using cover to conceal its swooping approach. Francolins and guinea-fowl are favourite prey of the African hawk-eagle but it also takes dassies, mongooses, hares and occasionally reptiles.

In the Park it is a widespread and common species, preferring woodland and avoiding open savanna and forested areas. It occurs singly or in pairs and is often seen soaring high above its territory. Breeding takes place in winter and only one chick normally survives from a two-egg clutch.

BROWN SNAKE-EAGLE

BATELEUR MALE

BROWN SNAKE-EAGLE
Circaetus cinereus
BRUINSLANGAREND

This medium-sized dark-brown eagle inhabits the wooded savanna and dry bushveld areas in the Park and is, as its name implies, adept at killing snakes. It prefers to hunt from a perch and is usually seen sitting alone on a tree or hilltop, scanning its surroundings for prey.

Although it will take lizards and (rarely) rodents, most of its prey consists of snakes. These are seized in the eagle's talons, close to the head, and killed by pummelling, crushing and pecking at the spine. The bird's legs are heavily scaled as a protection against snakebite. Strong digestive juices quickly denature the venom of snakes such as puff-adders and mambas – some of which may be up to three metres long.

BATELEUR
Terathopius ecaudatus
BERGHAAN

This magnificent eagle is arguably one of the supreme fliers found in African skies, gliding effortlessly for enormous distances with the minimum of wingbeats. It is a large bird with a very short tail, which makes it easily identifiable in flight. At close quarters it is equally unmistakable with its bright red legs, feet and face, and black, chestnut and grey plumage.

Bateleurs spend most of the day in flight, sweeping across country in great circles at low altitudes, scrutinizing the ground for potential prey. This consists of small- to medium-sized birds and mammals, reptiles, fish and carrion. Although rare outside protected areas, the bateleur is a relatively common resident of the Park.

AFRICAN FISH-EAGLE

LITTLE BANDED GOSHAWK

AFRICAN FISH-EAGLE
Haliaeetus vocifer
VISAREND

The African fish-eagle is unmistakable, with its white head, mantle and breast contrasting with the black wings and back and the chestnut abdomen. It is a very vocal eagle and for many people its characteristic loud ringing call is one of the most evocative sounds of the African bush.

Fish-eagles are widespread and relatively common in the Kruger National Park, especially along the perennial rivers. During the summer rains they may disperse to the many pools that form after rainstorms.

Their food consists primarily of fish up to one kilogram in weight and occasionally heavier. Although they catch most fish themselves, they will readily pirate fish from other birds.

LITTLE BANDED GOSHAWK
Accipiter badius
GEBANDE SPERWER

The little banded goshawk is an attractive and neatly featured bird of prey which occurs widely in the Park in savanna woodland and riverine bush habitats. It may be the most common hawk around water courses where large trees occur.

Small in size, usually weighing between 100 and 150 grams, this bird specializes in catching lizards which account for about 70 per cent of its diet, but also takes small birds, bats (at dusk), frogs, snakes and insects. The lizards are often seized while basking on rocks or the walls of buildings.

Little banded goshawks are solitary by nature and normally hunt from perches within the canopies of trees, swiftly pouncing on prey on the ground.

DARK CHANTING GOSHAWK

GYMNOGENE

DARK CHANTING GOSHAWK

Melierax metabates

DONKERSINGVALK

The dark chanting goshawk is a common resident of the Kruger National Park, favouring habitats such as thornveld and open savanna woodland. It appears to have a marked preference for dense bush regions, especially mopane and the virtually impenetrable Nyandu Bush of the north-eastern sandveld of the Park. Nevertheless it is a conspicuous bird as it often perches on solitary trees or other prominent objects on the landscape such as posts or stumps, from which vantage-points it scans the ground for prey.

Lizards appear to be the favoured prey but it will also take small birds, mammals and snakes as well as large insects. They have the dash and agility to overpower guinea-fowl, which weigh 1,2 kilograms compared to the dark chanting goshawk's mass of between 600 and 800 grams.

GYMNOGENE

Polyboroides typus

KAALWANGVALK

This medium-sized bird of prey is unusual both in its appearance and in its way of life. The gymnogene is one of the easiest birds of prey to identify; its breast, head and upperparts are grey, the long tail is black with a conspicuous white bar, and it has black-and-white barred underparts. The legs and the distinctive bare facial skin are yellow; the facial skin, however, flushes red during display.

This usually solitary bird is a common resident of dense woodland and woody kloofs in the Park, especially in the east. It is often seen scrambling about branches and tree-trunks or on the ground, with its wings flapping loosely, searching for birds, nestlings, eggs, small mammals, reptiles and amphibians. Its 'knee' joint is extraordinarily flexible, allowing the gymnogene to extract prey from holes in trees.

YELLOW-BILLED KITE

BLACK-SHOULDERED KITE

YELLOW-BILLED KITE

Milvus migrans parasitus
GEELBEKWOU

BLACK KITE

Milvus migrans migrans
SWARTWOU

The black kite – *Milvus migrans* is one of the most widespread of the world's birds of prey. Scientists recognize seven different subspecies of this bird and two of these, the black kite (subspecies *migrans*) of Eurasia, and the yellow-billed kite (subspecies *parasitus*) of equatorial Africa, are summer visitors to the Park.

Although the yellow-billed kite breeds in the Park, the black kite does not, only being here to avoid the northern winter. Both are large brown birds with a distinctly forked tail, but the black kite has a greyish head and black bill to the yellow-billed kite's brown head and yellow bill. They feed on most animal material, including carrion.

BLACK-SHOULDERED KITE

Elanus caeruleus
BLOUVALK

The black-shouldered kite is one of the most ubiquitous and best-known birds of prey in southern Africa. There can be few people who have not at some time seen this attractive little kite, which has an average mass of 250 grams, perched on a telephone-pole by the roadside or hovering stationary over open grassland. It is unmistakable with its red eyes, black bill, yellow legs, grey upperparts, black 'shoulders', white underparts, and short white tail.

It occurs throughout the Park, though is more common in the north than in the south. When rodent prey is plentiful, its numbers increase locally and it is certainly nomadic in that it is prepared to migrate to areas where prey is seasonably abundant. While usually solitary or in pairs, outside the breeding season the black-shouldered kite roosts communally.

COQUI FRANCOLIN
CRESTED FRANCOLIN

COQUI FRANCOLIN
Francolinus coqui
SWEMPIE

The coqui francolin is one of the smallest of southern Africa's 12 francolin species. It usually occurs in small coveys of four to six birds, occasionally up to 12. Both sexes have a yellowish or buff-coloured head with a contrasting darker crown and are thus distinguished from other francolins in southern Africa. The female has a white eyebrow and a white throat, both bordered by a thin black line. The belly of both sexes is heavily barred in black and white.

Coqui francolin are difficult to flush and usually crouch when disturbed. Once airborne they fly for a considerable distance before alighting again. They roost on the ground, sometimes in small groups, and they feed on insects, ticks and seeds which they find in their savanna woodland habitat. They occur almost throughout the Kruger National Park.

CRESTED FRANCOLIN
Francolinus sephaena
BOSPATRYS

This handsome, medium-sized francolin (with a mass of about 375 grams) is distinguishable from other francolins by its dark cap and contrasting broad white eyebrow stripe. Its breast is heavily streaked with black and the belly is finely barred. The upperwing feathers are a pale chocolate-brown, each feather adorned with a broad white stripe along the shaft.

Crested francolins occur in small coveys of six to 12 birds and are found in the Park in matted bush habitats, particularly near koppies, and along dry watercourses.

The crested francolin is not easily flushed, preferring to run rather than fly. It roosts in trees and is a noisy bird, especially at dusk and dawn. An interesting characteristic of this species is its habit of cocking its tail at a 45 degree angle. Its crest is only noticeable when it is alarmed.

NATAL FRANCOLIN

SWAINSON'S FRANCOLIN

NATAL FRANCOLIN
Francolinus natalensis
NATALSE FISANT

The Natal francolin has more or less uniform brown upperparts and black underparts, boldly barred and scaled with white. It has a red bill and red legs and may easily be distinguished from the crested francolin – the only other francolin in the Kruger National Park which has red legs – by its habit of holding the tail low.

It occurs widely throughout the Park, especially in riverine scrub and dense thickets along watercourses. It is very vocal at sunrise and sunset, its call being a harsh, strident crowing.

Although often seen in pairs, Natal francolins can form coveys of up to 10 birds. When flushed the covey members typically separate, but do not fly far, running into dense cover on landing. They roost in trees and feed on insects, molluscs, bulbs, fruit and seeds.

SWAINSON'S FRANCOLIN
Francolinus swainsonii
BOSVELDFISANT

This is the only francolin in the Kruger National Park which is brown above and below, albeit streaked with black. It is additionally distinguished by having black legs and feet, while the bare skin around its eyes and on its throat is red. It is a large francolin, males averaging 700 grams in mass and females 500 grams.

Swainson's francolin is very common in the Park, particularly in the central and northern regions, and shows a preference for bare overgrazed areas. Its broad habitat requirements are bushveld, grassveld with scattered woody vegetation, riverine bush and rank vegetation around vleis. Food items include seeds, berries, roots and bulbs as well as insects and even molluscs.

Coveys can consist of up to eight birds, but this species may also be seen alone or in pairs. At night it roosts in trees.

HELMETED GUINEA-FOWL

CRESTED GUINEA-FOWL

HELMETED GUINEA-FOWL

Numida meleagris

GEWONE TARENTAAL

Both species of southern African guinea-fowl occur in the Kruger National Park. Of the two, the helmeted guinea-fowl is the more common and occurs widespread throughout the whole of the Park. It is a medium-sized game-bird approximately 1,3 kilograms in mass, with the strong legs and large feet appropriate to a largely terrestrial way of life. The slate-grey plumage is finely spotted with white, the face and neck are naked and blue, and the naked crown is bright red. On the top of the head there is a vertical, horn-coloured bony casque.

This gregarious species roosts in trees at night and feeds on insects, ticks, seeds, bulbs and berries. It favours open woodland, grassland and thorn-tree habitats.

CRESTED GUINEA-FOWL

Guttera pucherani

KUIFKOPTARENTAAL

The crested guinea-fowl is similar in general appearance to the helmeted guinea-fowl, but instead of a bony casque on the top of its head it has a tuft of curly black feathers. It has a crimson iris but otherwise there is no red on the head. The bare skin of the face and upper neck is slate-grey and the fold of skin between the gape and the back of the neck is white.

It is far more secretive than the helmeted guinea-fowl and favours habitats that provide dense vegetation cover such as the matted thickets at the edge of evergreen forests, ironwood groves or gallery forest. In the Kruger National Park these conditions are met near Pafuri, Shipudza, Punda Maria and Nwanetsi.

AFRICAN FINFOOT FEMALE

BLACK CRAKE

AFRICAN FINFOOT
Podica senegalensis
WATERTRAPPER

The African finfoot is an aquatic bird somewhat similar in appearance to the darter (but with a shorter and stouter neck) or to a cormorant (but with a red bill, red legs and feet, and a distinctive white stripe down the side of the neck from behind the eye). This dark-brown bird is not commonly seen, being retiring in its ways, and often swimming close to the river-banks beneath overhanging vegetation.

The finfoot characteristically swims low in the water, propelling itself with its lobed (not webbed) feet as it forages for its prey of insects, crabs, snails, frogs and fish. In the Park it is a fairly common resident of the Luvuvhu and Sabie rivers and has been recorded on all rivers except the Crocodile.

BLACK CRAKE
Amaurornis flavirostris
SWARTRIETHAAN

This attractive little bird, about the size of a small dove, is an unmistakable resident of the Park, being seen singly, in pairs or in small groups in marshes, quiet back-waters and the reedy vegetation around permanent dams. Its plumage is pitch-black, with a conspicuous yellow bill and bright-red eyes, legs and feet. It has long, widely spread toes which support it on marshy ground and aquatic vegetation.

Although not easily seen because of the nature of its habitat, it is not shy and ventures into the open at dawn and dusk. It is a fast runner and a good swimmer, but is a reluctant flier. Prey items consist of insects, crustaceans, molluscs, small fish, seeds, water-plants and even herons' eggs.

PHOTO ACCESS/TERRY CAREW

PHOTO ACCESS/LEX HES

KORI BUSTARD

BLACK-BELLIED KORHAAN

KORI BUSTARD
Ardeotis kori
GOMPOU

The kori bustard is the world's largest flying bird, with a standing height to the top of its head of just more than a metre, and a mass of around 15 kilograms. Specimens of over 18 kilograms have been recorded. A greyish-brown bird, it has a white belly and a finely barred neck. There is a distinct crest at the back of the head.

These magnificent birds are widespread in the Park, favouring areas of dry thornveld and open grassland. Usually seen alone or in pairs, outside the breeding season they may occur in flocks of up to 40 birds.

The cock is renowned for his spectacular courtship display during which he fans out his feathers and inflates his neck to an extraordinary degree.

BLACK-BELLIED KORHAAN
Eupodotis melanogaster
LANGBEENKORHAAN

This medium-sized bustard is similar in general appearance to the red-crested korhaan but is larger, with longer legs and a long, thin neck. Although both species have black underparts, in the black-bellied korhaan the black does not stop at the breast but continues as a narrow line up the front of the neck to the chin.

It occurs widely throughout the Kruger National Park preferring low bush areas, especially in the north; it does, however, become more common in the south of the Park in summer. It is usually seen singly or in pairs. Like the red-crested korhaan it is difficult to flush, staying motionless and relying on camouflage when the threat of danger arises.

RED-CRESTED KORHAAN

AFRICAN JACANA

RED-CRESTED KORHAAN
Eupodotis ruficrista
BOSKORHAAN

The red-crested korhaan is one of the smaller of the southern African bustards, having a bill-tip to tail-tip length of about 50 centimetres. It has a distinctive black belly and breast, predominantly buff back with numerous black and cream chevrons, and creamy-white legs and feet. It could be confused with the black-bellied korhaan, but in the latter species the black coloration of the belly extends as a line up the foreneck to the throat in the male.

Usually solitary or in pairs, the red-crested korhaan inhabits savanna and bushveld habitats and is difficult to see in tall grass, relying as it does on immobility and its excellent camouflage for concealment. It feeds on arthropods, seeds and fruit.

AFRICAN JACANA
Actophilornis africanus
GROOTLANGTOON

This distinctive, bantam-sized, long-legged bird is an inhabitant of pans, vleis and quiet river waters throughout the Park. It has a rich chestnut body, black hindneck, golden-yellow breast, white foreneck and blue frontal shield. The African jacana is sometimes called the 'lily-trotter' because it has extraordinarily elongated toes and claws which enable it to walk easily on flimsy floating plants such as water-lilies, its mass of some 250 grams being distributed over a wide area.

It swims and dives well, a skill which is particularly important during the period of wing-moult when it is flightless. It eats insects, molluscs, crustaceans and seeds and usually occurs in small loose flocks.

PHOTO ACCESS/J&B PHOTOGRAPHERS

PHOTO ACCESS/TERRY CAREW

THREE-BANDED PLOVER

BLACKSMITH PLOVER

THREE-BANDED PLOVER
Charadrius tricollaris
DRIEBANDSTRANDKIEWIET

The three-banded plover is an attractive small bird occurring along the shorelines of the smaller waterbodies in the Kruger National Park and is easily recognizable by the two prominent black bands across its breast, separated by a white band, and by the red or vermilion eye-ring.

These birds feed entirely on animal food such as insects, crustaceans, molluscs and worms which they probe out of the mud at the water's edge with their bills. Typically they run in short bursts, stopping now and again to jab rapidly at the mud, in search of their prey.

During the breeding season from June to October they are seen in pairs near their nests, which are simply shallow scrapes ringed with stones in the gravel or mud near water. After the breeding season they are found in loose flocks of up to 40 birds.

BLACKSMITH PLOVER
Vanellus armatus
BONTKIEWIET

This handsome plover is unlikely to be confused with any other bird. It has a greyish back and wings, black underparts and face, and a distinctive white crown extending over the forehead. It obtains its name from its call – a *'tink-tink-tink'* sound rather like a hammer on an anvil.

The blacksmith plover is a common resident of the Kruger National Park north of the Olifants River and is occasionally seen as a vagrant to the south of the river. Its favoured habitats are the shorelines of dams, pans and vleis, and wet grasslands, where it feeds on insects, worms, molluscs and other invertebrates.

Breeding occurs throughout the year although there is a peak of activity in September; clutches usually consist of three or four eggs. Non-breeding birds congregate in loose flocks of 20 to 30 birds.

76

CROWNED PLOVER

SPOTTED DIKKOP

CROWNED PLOVER
Vanellus coronatus
KROONKIEWIET

The crowned plover is one of the best-known birds in South Africa, familiar both to farmer and to city-dweller – the bane of the insomniac because of its strident cry, emitted by day and by night at the first sign of disturbance. It is unmistakable in appearance with its red legs and feet, red bill (black at the tip), yellow eyes, and black crown encircled by first a white band and then a black band.

These birds favour short dry grassland, overgrazed or burnt veld and lightly wooded savanna, and are found over the whole of the Park. City playing-fields, parks and gardens mimic these habitats, and crowned plovers have adapted well to suburban life. They defend their nests by noisily dive-bombing intruders and often feign injury in order to lure potential predators away from their young.

SPOTTED DIKKOP
Burhinus capensis
DIKKOP

The spotted dikkop is a medium-sized, long-legged bird, which is rather plover-like in appearance and behaviour. Indeed it shares the crowned plover's fondness for grassy fields and parks in cities and is well known to most South Africans with its loud piping calls at night. Its large yellow eyes are a conspicuous identifying feature. It could perhaps be confused with the water dikkop, but its wings are spotted dark brown on buff and lack the water dikkop's pale grey wing-bar which is edged above with a narrow white line.

Although it is mostly active at dusk, dawn and during the night, the spotted dikkop may also be seen on overcast days. Its food consists of insects, crustaceans, molluscs, frogs and even grass seeds. In the Park it favours open grassland areas and is particularly common around Satara Rest Camp.

WATER DIKKOP   DOUBLE-BANDED SANDGROUSE

WATER DIKKOP
Burhinus vermiculatus
WATERDIKKOP

Although superficially similar in appearance to the spotted dikkop, the water dikkop is distinguished by its green iris and by its conspicuous pale-grey wing-bar edged with a white line; the spotted dikkop has a bright yellow iris and has uniform buff wings spotted with dark brown. The two species also have different preferences of habitat, the spotted dikkop preferring open grassland not necessarily near water, while the water dikkop is found only in the vicinity of water.

In the Park it is less common and less widespread than the spotted dikkop, but occurs in suitable habitats north of the Sabie River. Its food consists of snails, shellfish and insects. Although it is essentially nocturnal, it is often active by day and its strident piping calls can be heard both at night and during the day.

DOUBLE-BANDED SANDGROUSE
Pterocles bicinctus
DUBBELBANDSANDPATRYS

The double-banded sandgrouse is a small, short-legged, ground-living bird about the size of a Cape turtle dove. The male has bold black-and-white bars on the forehead and two contiguous breast-bands, the upper white and lower black. The female is less conspicuous than the male and is finely barred above and below.

These interesting little birds are common residents of the Kruger National Park, particularly from Tshokwane northwards, and occur in acacia and similar savanna, dry bushveld and mopane woodland. During the day they lie up in the shade of rocks or vegetation, in pairs or in small groups, but after dusk they are highly gregarious and congregate in flocks of hundreds of birds to fly to water. They feed on small dry seeds and can often be seen foraging at the side of the road.

MOURNING DOVE

CAPE TURTLE DOVE

MOURNING DOVE
Streptopelia decipiens
ROOIOOGTORTELDUIF

This attractive dove is confined in South Africa to the subtropical northern Transvaal and Transvaal Lowveld. It is found at localities along the entire length of the Park and is particularly common at Pafuri, Letaba, Satara and Lower Sabie. The mourning dove is similar in appearance to the Cape turtle dove, both being generally greyish with a half-collar of black on the hindneck, but can be distinguished by a conspicuous ring of red skin around the eye. It is slightly smaller than the red-eyed dove, and differs from that species in having white ends to its outer tail feathers; there is no white on the tail of the red-eyed dove.

Mourning doves have a characteristic bubbling 'wuwu-woo' call, dropping in pitch on the 'woo'. They feed on seeds and although they occur in pairs, they flock together to drink around sunrise and sunset.

CAPE TURTLE DOVE
Streptopelia capicola
GEWONE TORTELDUIF

The Cape turtle dove is perhaps the most common dove in South Africa and probably also the most numerous in the Kruger National Park. It occurs throughout the Park in savanna woodland, even in mopane country, but is absent from densely forested areas. This medium-sized dove is similar to the mourning dove, red-eyed dove and laughing dove, but differs from the first two in not having red skin around the eye and from the laughing dove by the black half-collar on the hindneck.

It forages on the ground for seeds, insects and winged termites, but seeks the shelter of trees for resting. Although occasionally found singly or in pairs, the Cape turtle dove is commonly seen in large flocks, especially at water-holes. Its call is very well known – a high-pitched and repetitive 'kuk-KOORR-ru'.

LAUGHING DOVE

GREEN-SPOTTED DOVE

LAUGHING DOVE

Streptopelia senegalensis

ROOIBORSDUIF

This dove must be familiar to most South Africans as it occurs all over the Republic. It is easily distinguished from the other turtle dove species of the genus *Streptopelia* as it has a cinnamon-coloured breast spotted with black, a pinkish head and lacks the half-collar of black on the hindneck.

Like the Cape turtle dove, the laughing dove is a common species in the Kruger National Park, occurring in a wide range of savanna and open woodland habitats as well as in the rest-camps. It is, however, not as tolerant of arid conditions as the Cape turtle dove. During the wet summer months the Park's population of laughing doves is supplemented by immigration from outside.

The call of the laughing dove is a bubbling descent of six or eight notes with a certain laughing quality – '*koo koo kuRUkutu-koo*'.

GREEN-SPOTTED DOVE

Turtur chalcospilos

GROENVLEKDUIF

This small dove occurs widespread through the Park's various woodland habitats. Although it can be found in thornveld and dry broad-leaved woodland, it tends to favour the more heavily wooded areas along watercourses. It has cinnamon-coloured wings with several metallic-green spots and it has two dark bands enclosing a pale band across the lower back.

The green-spotted dove feeds on the ground, on seeds, berries and winged termites when available. When disturbed, it takes off with a loud wing-clap, darting off with a rapid zigzagging flight.

Its call is one of the characteristic sounds of the bushveld and is a long, mournful and monotonous series of notes – '*du, du... du, du... du... du, du... dudu, du, du, du, du, du, du*', starting off slowly and speeding up towards the end.

BROWN-HEADED PARROT

CAPE PARROT

BROWN-HEADED PARROT
Poicephalus cryptoxanthus
BRUINKOPPAPEGAAI

Parrots are relatively scarce in Africa, with only 15 species all told, of which eight occur in southern Africa. Of the two species found in the Kruger National Park, the brown-headed parrot is more widespread, being found in woodland and riverine forest in all regions of the Park.

It is only two-thirds the size of the Cape parrot and has a more greenish plumage and a brown head and neck. In flight it shows a conspicuous yellow underwing, absent on the Cape parrot, and there is no red on the head nor on the bend of the wing, as in the Cape parrot.

It is a gregarious, noisy bird, usually occurring in small flocks, but hard to see in the dense foliage of trees where it forages for fruit, flowers, nectar, seeds and nuts. Its call is a typical strident, metallic 'chree-oo, chree-oo, KREEK'.

CAPE PARROT
Poicephalus robustus
GROOTPAPEGAAI

The Cape parrot is a large dull-green bird with distinctive red patches on the forehead, the leading edge of the wing (the 'shoulder') and the lower part of the thigh. It has a restricted distribution in the Kruger National Park, being found only in the north. It is fairly common around Punda Maria, and during the dry season it tends to be confined to the riverine forest of the Pafuri area.

The bill of the Cape parrot is strong, curved and pointed at the tip. It is used to grip branches as the bird clambers about in the trees while foraging, and also to crack open hard fruit kernels. Berries and figs also form part of the parrot's diet. Although this rather scarce and interesting bird is gregarious – normally being seen in flocks of up to 12 birds – it roosts singly. Its call consists of loud, harsh squawks and screeches.

GREY LOURIE   PURPLE-CRESTED LOURIE

GREY LOURIE
Corythaixoides concolor
KWÊVOËL

The grey lourie is a well-known and unmistakable resident of the Kruger National Park, occurring all over wherever suitable open bushveld and savanna exist, but shunning the low mopane areas of the north. Its appearance is distinctive, with its plain, wholly grey plumage, rounded floppy wings and conspicuous crest, as is its call – a harsh, drawn-out, somewhat nasal 'go 'way' (hence its other popular name, the 'go-away bird'). It produces various other yowls and shrieks. Seen from a distance or in silhouette, the grey lourie may appear rather like a large mousebird.

Although a clumsy flier, it is quick and agile in trees where it forages for fruit and flowers, birds, insects and nestling birds.

PURPLE-CRESTED LOURIE
Tauraco porphyreolophus
BLOUKUIFLOERIE

This extremely attractive and relatively large bird, with a length of about 40 centimetres is a common breeding resident, and is essentially an inhabitant of riverine forest habitats in the Kruger National Park. It occurs in pairs or in small groups and forages for fruit in the canopy of trees with great agility.

Although it is a shy and secretive bird and will sit motionless in a tree for extended periods until disturbed, an observer may occasionally be rewarded with a view of the purple-crested lourie as it leaps or glides from one tree to another, displaying its richly crimson wings, green body, and iridescent purple wing-coverts and crest. Its call is a loud 'kok-kok-kok-kok'.

BURCHELL'S COUCAL

BURCHELL'S COUCAL

Centropus superciliosus
GEWONE VLEILOERIE

This medium to large bird (length around 40 centimetres) is easily recognizable with its black cap and mantle, creamy-white underparts, black tail and chestnut wings. Its call is one of the characteristic sounds of the bushveld: being a series of around 17 liquid hooting notes reminiscent of the sound of water gurgling out of a narrow-necked bottle – '*du-du-du-du... du-du*' – falling at first and rising at the end.

Although it is widespread throughout the Park, Burchell's coucal shows a preference for the rank and dense vegetation associated with riverine bush or the edges of streams and marshes, where it clambers around, alone or in pairs, searching for its prey of insects, snails, lizards, frogs, mice and birds' eggs and nestlings.

KLAAS'S CUCKOO MALE

DIEDERIK CUCKOO IMMATURE

KLAAS'S CUCKOO
Chrysococcyx klaas
MEITJIE

Eleven members of the family Cuculidae occur in the Kruger National Park, comprising nine species of cuckoo and two coucal. Klaas's cuckoo is a particularly attractive representative of the family and is found in woodland habitats in the Park throughout the year.

It may be confused with the diederik cuckoo, but has a duller coloration, no white on the wings and has a dark brown eye. The male is distinctively metallic-green above and on the sides of its breast, and white below, while the female is brownish above with green barring on the wings.

At least 22 species of passerine birds act as unwitting hosts to this brood parasite, from flycatchers to sunbirds.

DIEDERIK CUCKOO
Chrysococcyx caprius
DIEDERIK

Named for its persistent, plaintive musical call, '*dee-dee-deederik*', this small iridescent-green bird resembles Klaas's cuckoo but has a long white eyebrow stripe and prominent white spots on the wings; the male Klaas's cuckoo has only a small white patch behind the eye and does not have white markings on the wings.

The diederik cuckoo is an intra-African migrant from tropical Africa and is present in the Park from October to April, favouring woodland, savanna and riverine bush. It is the most common of the summer-visiting glossy cuckoos in southern Africa.

At least 24 species of small birds are parasitized by this cuckoo in the region. Only one egg is laid per host nest.

BARN OWL

MARSH OWL

BARN OWL
Tyto alba
NONNETJIE-UIL

The barn owl has a world-wide distribution and it is probably the most widely distributed of all land-bird species, occurring over the whole of the Park, wherever suitable nesting- and roosting-sites exist: these include holes in trees, rock crevices and even hamerkop nests.

During the day the barn owl hides in a suitable cavity, from which it emerges at dusk to seek its prey of rats, mice, shrews, small birds, lizards, frogs and insects. It flies silently and can catch its prey in total darkness using hearing alone.

It can be a prolific breeder in years of rodent population 'explosions', when clutch-sizes are increased from a normal five eggs to as many as 12 eggs.

MARSH OWL
Asio capensis
VLEI-UIL

The marsh owl is a medium-sized 'typical' owl, brown in colour with a paler face margined in black. Its bill is black and the brown eyes are surrounded by blackish feathers which make them appear larger. It has short 'ear'-tufts (unconnected with hearing) situated on the forehead.

The favoured habitats of the marsh owl include vleis, grassland and the edges of marshes where it can be seen hunting at night, although also often on cloudy days. Prey consists of rodents, insects, small birds, shrews and frogs. It is the only gregarious southern African owl and groups of up to 40 are on record. In the Park it only occurs commonly on the Hlamalala Flats east of Punda Maria.

PEARL-SPOTTED OWL

SCOPS OWL

PEARL-SPOTTED OWL
Glaucidium perlatum
WITKOLUIL

This diminutive bird is the smallest owl in southern Africa with a length of between 18 and 19 centimetres. (The laughing dove measures about 25 centimetres.) It has a disproportionately large, rounded, 'puffball' head, and is brown above, dotted with pearl-like white spots. It has no 'ear'-tufts. A curious feature of the pearl-spotted owl is the 'false face' on the back of the head, formed by two patches of dark feathers – the 'eyes' – each framed in white.

Although it is mainly nocturnal in habit, it can be active by day and takes little trouble to conceal itself. It often perches in leafy trees from where it drops on its prey of insects, rodents, bats, lizards and birds. It occurs throughout the Park.

SCOPS OWL
Otus senegalensis
SKOPSUIL

The scops owl is a tiny owl, not much bigger than the pearl-spotted owl. It is, however, clearly distinguishable from the latter by having long 'ear'-tufts. The scops owl occurs in two colour forms, grey and brown; both forms, however, have a grey face, a feature which clearly distinguishes this species from the appropriately named white-faced owl, the only other small owl in the Park with prominent 'ear'-tufts.

It is marvellously camouflaged during the day, resting motionless against a tree-trunk. When disturbed, it closes its yellow eyes, raises its 'ears' and elongates its body, becoming almost indistinguishable from a dead branch. It is widespread in wooded areas in the Park, particularly in the south.

SPOTTED EAGLE-OWL   GIANT EAGLE-OWL

SPOTTED EAGLE-OWL
Bubo africanus
GEVLEKTE OORUIL

This large nocturnal owl, which has an average length of 45 centimetres, is the most common – and the smallest – of South Africa's three eagle-owls, all of which occur in the Kruger National Park. They all have 'ear'-tufts but the spotted eagle-owl may be distinguished by its light underparts, barred with dark grey and spotted with brown on the breast. The giant eagle-owl has barred underparts with no spots, while the Cape eagle-owl has heavy dark-brown blotches on the underparts.

The spotted eagle-owl can be found throughout the Park in woodland and savanna, but shows a distinct preference for rocky areas. It feeds on insects, reptiles, birds and mammals.

GIANT EAGLE-OWL
Bubo lacteus
REUSE-OORUIL

The giant eagle-owl is the largest owl in Africa with a length of around 60 centimetres. Although it has 'ear'-tufts, they are less conspicuous than those of the other two eagle-owl species of South Africa. It may be identified by its large size, its pale sepia-grey upperparts, and its finely barred grey and white underparts. Unlike the other eagle-owls which have yellow or orange eyes, it has dark-brown eyes – and pink upper eyelids.

This predominantly nocturnal owl appears to prefer areas with large trees and may be more widespread in the south than in the north of the Park. Its prey includes secretary-birds, monkeys, mice, snakes, lizards, frogs, fish, insects and scorpions.

FIERY-NECKED NIGHTJAR

MOZAMBIQUE NIGHTJAR

FIERY-NECKED NIGHTJAR
Caprimulgus pectoralis
AFRIKA-NAGUIL

Six species of nightjar are found in the Park. These small birds are all very similar in appearance and behaviour, and are difficult to tell apart in the field. Like its fellows, the fiery-necked nightjar, has an elaborately patterned plumage comprised of black, white, rufous and various shades of brown. The rich rufous collar and breast distinguish it from other nightjars.

It is crepuscular (active in twilight) and also nocturnal, lying up during the day on shady ground, protected by its excellent camouflage. Insects (especially beetles) and spiders constitute its prey; it hunts by hawking from a favourite perch in a tree. Its well-known call has been rendered as '*Good Lord deliver us*'.

MOZAMBIQUE NIGHTJAR
Caprimulgus fossii
LAEVELDNAGUIL

The Mozambique nightjar is one of the more common nightjars of the Lowveld, but it is difficult to distinguish from the other five nightjar species found in the Park. It favours scrub areas with open sandy ground in savanna. Its call is a high-pitched frog-like trill, which has also been compared to a gurgling engine. The call varies in pitch, and volume.

Like other nightjars, the Mozambique nightjar is crepuscular, being most active at dusk when it hunts for its insect prey of termites, beetles, moths and ants by hawking from a perch or by flying over ground or water in longer sallies. It may often be seen just after dusk sitting in clearings or on gravel roads.

SPECKLED MOUSEBIRD

RED-FACED MOUSEBIRD

SPECKLED MOUSEBIRD
Colius striatus
GEVLEKTE MUISVOËL

Both the speckled mousebird (or coly) and the red-faced mousebird occur in the Park. These fruit-eating birds are easily recognizable with their long tails – about twice as long as their bodies – and their distinctive feathered crests. The speckled mousebird is a widespread, gregarious and arboreal resident of the Park, tending to favour bushveld habitats and tangled thickets where it may be seen clambering about in the branches in flocks of five to 20 birds, searching for fruit, leaves, seeds and nectar.

It is almost uniform brown in colour with a black bill and face and is thus easily distinguished from the red-faced mousebird which has blue-grey plumage with a patch of bare red skin on the face.

RED-FACED MOUSEBIRD
Colius indicus
ROOIWANGMUISVOËL

The most widespread of the three mousebird species in South Africa is the red-faced mousebird. It occurs throughout the Park in savanna with thickets and in riverine bush. It is very similar in appearance to the speckled mousebird, which is also a resident of the Park, but can be immediately recognized by its red patch of bare facial skin and more blue-grey plumage.

Like other mousebirds, the red-faced mousebird is gregarious by nature, usually occurring in flocks of up to eight birds, occasionally more. It is considered to be more wary than its cousins, flying high and fast from one feeding area to the next. Breeding takes place during the summer months in the Kruger National Park.

PIED KINGFISHER MALE

GIANT KINGFISHER MALE

PIED KINGFISHER
Ceryle rudis
BONTVISVANGER

This handsome bird is one of nine species of kingfisher occurring in the Kruger National Park and is the most widespread of its family in South Africa. The pied kingfisher is distinctively coloured in black and white only and although the sexes are similar, the male has two black breast-bands while the female has one, which is usually broken in the middle.

Pied kingfishers will eat crustaceans and insects, but their main prey consists of small fish weighing up to two grams. As they are relatively tame they can be watched at close quarters as they hunt from a perch or hover over the water before plunging in head-first, wings folded back, to seize the prey.

GIANT KINGFISHER
Ceryle maxima
REUSEVISVANGER

The largest of South Africa's kingfishers is the giant kingfisher, with a length of almost 45 centimetres from bill-tip to tail-tip, and a mass of around 350 grams. In the Kruger National Park, it is commonly seen at dams or along wooded streams.

The giant kingfisher is readily identified by its size, heavy black bill, black back finely spotted with white, and white-streaked black crest. The male has a chestnut breast and a black-spotted white belly, while the female has a black-spotted white breast and chestnut belly.

Unlike the pied kingfisher, it rarely hovers over water, preferring to dive straight from its perch to catch its prey of fish and, more rarely, crabs and frogs.

HALF-COLLARED KINGFISHER

MALACHITE KINGFISHER

HALF-COLLARED KINGFISHER
Alcedo semitorquata
BLOUVISVANGER

This smallish kingfisher with its cobalt-blue upperparts can be separated from other 'blue' kingfishers in South Africa by its distinctly black bill, the others having red bills, and by the blue 'half-collar' on the sides of the upper breast. It also has a white throat, a white patch on each side of its hindneck, rich buff underparts, and red or orange legs and feet.

It is not as common as some of the other kingfishers and in the Kruger National Park occurs along wooded streams, especially in the south along the Sabie River. Although it will occasionally hover, it normally hunts by perching low over water before plunging in to catch its prey which consists of small fish or crabs.

MALACHITE KINGFISHER
Alcedo cristata
KUIFKOPVISVANGER

The malachite kingfisher and the pygmy kingfisher are the two smallest kingfishers in the Park and perhaps the most beautiful. Both have scarlet bills, legs and feet, bright deep-blue upperparts, a white throat and orange-chestnut underparts. The blue-and-black barred crown of the malachite kingfisher, however, extends down to the eye and has a turquoise tinge; the pygmy kingfisher, which prefers a woodland to a waterside habitat, has a blue-and-black crown which is separated from the eye by a broad chestnut eyebrow.

The malachite kingfisher frequents quiet waters in the Park, where it catches fish, insects, tadpoles and crustaceans by diving from a low branch at the water's edge.

PHOTO ACCESS/ATHOL FRANZ STUDIO

PHOTO ACCESS/LEX HES

BROWN-HOODED KINGFISHER
Halcyon albiventris
BRUINKOPVISVANGER

It is a common misconception that all king-fishers eat fish: many species are in fact virtually independent of water and hunt invertebrate and vertebrate prey in wood-land. The brown-hooded kingfisher, found in most parts of the Park excepting the mopane veld in the north, is one such. It is a medium-sized kingfisher, and has a dis-tinctly brown crown, a black (male) or brown (female) upper back and wings, blue flight-feathers, and buffy-white underparts; the legs and feet are red, as is the black-tipped bill.

. This kingfisher eats mainly insects, but also lizards, rodents, snakes and small birds which are caught in a swift pounce from a perch on a branch.

WOODLAND KINGFISHER
Halcyon senegalensis
BOSVELDVISVANGER

As its name suggests, the woodland king-fisher is another of the non-aquatic king-fishers. It is a breeding intra-African migrant which arrives in the Park during the first weeks of November and departs in late April or May. Although it prefers the woodland habitat along (sometimes dry) watercourses, its can also be encountered in denser savanna away from water. Its prey consists of insects, lizards, snakes, frogs and occasionally fish.

The woodland kingfisher is a striking bird with its whitish head, bright light-blue upperparts, black eye-stripe, black patch on the bend of the wing and the 'two-tone' bill, red above and black below. (The similar mangrove kingfisher has an all-red bill.)

STRIPED KINGFISHER

CARMINE BEE-EATER

STRIPED KINGFISHER
Halcyon chelicuti
GESTREEPTE VISVANGER

The diminutive striped kingfisher is another non-aquatic, mainly insectivorous kingfisher. It is a common resident species in the Park favouring parkland areas of bushveld, but is absent from forest and very dry thornveld.

Compared to other kingfishers it is somewhat sombre in colour, with a brown back, black-and-white streaked crown and a white collar round the neck. Its bright-blue upper tail-coverts are only noticeable in flight. It is the only kingfisher in southern Africa with a bill which is black above and red below. (The woodland kingfisher's bill is red above and black below.)

The striped kingfisher watches for its prey from a perch on a branch.

CARMINE BEE-EATER
Merops rubicoides
ROOIBORSDYVRETER

Of the six South African species of bee-eater, five occur in the Kruger National Park. These brightly plumaged, graceful birds subsist entirely on insects which are caught in mid-air after a graceful swooping pursuit, often with much twisting and turning. The carmine bee-eater is particularly attractive. Its rose-red upper- and underparts contrast effectively with the blue crown and undertail-coverts and green rump; the central tail-feathers are considerably elongated.

It is a non-breeding visitor to the Kruger National Park from December to March when large flocks of hundreds of birds can be seen, sometimes in the company of other bee-eater species.

EUROPEAN BEE-EATER

WHITE-FRONTED BEE-EATER

EUROPEAN BEE-EATER
Merops apiaster
EUROPESE BYVRETER

This migrant from Eurasia and North Africa arrives in South Africa in September and departs for the northern hemisphere in March/April. Its coloration is striking, with its yellow throat, blue underparts and whitish forehead shading back over the crown to turquoise and chestnut; it is the only South African bee-eater species to have a chestnut crown and back.

This gregarious bird has a characteristic liquid trilling call, '*kwirriri*', and is often seen in flocks perched on telephone wires or in trees. Its prey of bees, wasps, dragonflies and other insects is normally caught in flight in graceful swooping forays from a perch. It is a common non-breeding visitor to the Park during the summer months.

WHITE-FRONTED BEE-EATER
Merops bullockoides
ROOIKEELBYVRETER

The name 'white-fronted bee-eater' is misleading in that the white is confined to the forehead and to a narrow band on the upper throat or chin. The lower throat is bright red and this combination of red and white on the throat is diagnostic for the species. The upperparts and wings are green, the breast is cinnamon and the undertail-coverts are bright blue. It does not have elongated central tail-feathers, unlike some of the other bee-eater species.

This bee-eater roosts communally at night, but it disperses into small groups during the day. It feeds on butterflies. In the Kruger National Park it is a common resident species but is confined to the vicinity of the large perennial rivers.

LITTLE BEE-EATER

EUROPEAN ROLLER

LITTLE BEE-EATER
Merops pusillus
KLEINBYVRETER

This species is the smallest of the six South African bee-eaters and with a bill- to tail-tip length of only 17 or 18 centimetres it is only half the size of the carmine bee-eater. It has a squared-off tail – as does the larger white-fronted bee eater – but the end of the tail has a diagnostic black band. The plumage is green and yellow overall, and the throat is yellow, bordered below by a black upper breast patch, and the underparts are an orange-buff colour.

The little bee-eater is normally seen alone or in pairs. It is a common breeding resident of the Park and occurs in bushveld and savanna habitats. It nests solitarily, excavating a burrow in a low bank, aardvark hole or in level ground.

EUROPEAN ROLLER
Coracias garrulus
EUROPESE TROUPANT

All five southern African rollers can be seen in the Park. These brightly coloured birds all have blue, lilac or purple in their plumage and are named for their rolling, somersaulting display flights.

The European roller is a non-breeding summer visitor from Europe and western Asia. It arrives here in early summer and departs in April. Unlike the other rollers it has no lilac or purple coloration, its head and underparts being a light sky-blue and its upperparts brown. It is distinguished from the racket-tailed roller and the lilac-breasted roller, which both have long tail-feathers, by its short square-ended tail. This usually solitary species feeds on flying termites, beetles, locusts and bees.

LILAC-BREASTED ROLLER

HOOPOE

LILAC-BREASTED ROLLER
Coracias caudata

The lilac-breasted roller is the only one of the region's roller species to have a lilac throat and breast and a blue belly. Its blue tail is forked and markedly elongated, its crown is light green and its back is light brown. Its bright-blue wings are most noticeable in flight.

This breeding resident of the Park prefers open woodland habitats, particularly in the north. It occurs singly or in pairs and is often seen perched on the top of a tree or bush from which vantage-point it flies to the ground to procure its prey of insects, scorpions, centipedes, snails, frogs, snakes, lizards, small birds and rodents. Insects disturbed by game animals or flushed by grass-fires are often taken in flight.

HOOPOE
Upupa epops

This bird is well known throughout South Africa and is quite unmistakable with its cinnamon-coloured plumage and crest. Its wings are boldly barred in black and white and the brown bill is long and slightly curved. The black-tipped crest is normally directed backwards but is raised fan-like when the bird is alarmed.

The hoopoe is found throughout the Park in savanna and open woodland, usually seen walking with quick steps and nodding head as it probes for insects, earthworms, cutworms and even small snakes and frogs. Its flight is heavy and slow and has been described as butterfly-like. Breeding takes place in spring and two or three broods may be raised each season.

TRUMPETER HORNBILL

GREY HORNBILL MALE

TRUMPETER HORNBILL

Bycanistes bucinator

GEWONE BOSKRAAI

All seven of the hornbill species occurring in South Africa can be found in the Kruger National Park. They are unmistakable birds with massive, downward-curving bills which in most species are topped by a horny casque.

The trumpeter hornbill is one of those with a casque on the bill. It is about the size of a crow and is mainly black in colour but with a white belly and white on the tips of the secondary wing-feathers and on the tips of the outer tail-feathers. There is a bare patch of skin around the eye.

Often revealed first by its trumpeting or wailing call, it occurs along the Park's perennial rivers, where it forages in the trees for fruit (especially figs) and insects.

GREY HORNBILL

Tockus nasutus

GRYSNEUSHORINGVOËL

This medium-sized hornbill is relatively common in the northern districts of the Kruger National Park, where it occurs in savanna and bushveld habitats. As its name suggests, it is a dull-greyish colour, but it has a whitish abdomen, a whitish eyebrow stripe and mottled brown and dark-brown wings. The male's bill is larger than the female's and is blackish with a cream wedge-shaped patch below the casque at the base of the upper jaw. The female's bill has a yellow upper jaw while its lower jaw is red and black.

The grey hornbill's diet comprises insects, rodents, frogs, chamaeleons and fruit. It prefers to forage in trees rather than on the ground and often takes insects in flight.

YELLOW-BILLED HORNBILL

RED-BILLED HORNBILL

YELLOW-BILLED HORNBILL
Tockus flavirostris
GEELBEKNEUSHORINGVOËL

This widespread resident of dry savanna bush and mopane habitats in the Kruger National Park is commonly seen around rest-camps and along roadsides. It is very popular with visitors to the Park, who often have a grandstand view of its antics as it runs along the ground searching for its prey of rodents, insects, scorpions, centipedes and seeds. It may occur singly, in pairs or in small groups.

The large yellow-orange bill is diagnostic for the species. It could possibly be confused in this respect with that of the female grey hornbill, whose upper bill only is yellow. However, the yellow-billed hornbill's boldly mottled black-and-white wings should settle the identification.

RED-BILLED HORNBILL
Tockus erythrorhynchus
ROOIBEKNEUSHORINGVOËL

Slightly smaller than the yellow-billed hornbill, the red-billed hornbill can be clearly distinguished from the latter by its all-red bill, which does not have a casque. Its wings are mottled boldly in black and white. The crowned hornbill also has a red bill but can be differentiated by its obvious casque and the plumage of its upperparts, which is black.

This fairly tame species occurs widely through the Kruger National Park in savanna and mopane woodland, especially in dry and overgrazed regions. Its diet is recorded as consisting of seeds, insects, scorpions and weaver-bird eggs. Like most other hornbills, the female seals herself into her nesting-hole in a tree to incubate her eggs.

GROUND HORNBILL   LESSER STRIPED SWALLOW

PETER STEYN

PETER STEYN

GROUND HORNBILL
Bucorvus leadbeateri
BROMVOËL

This turkey-sized hornbill is unmistakable, with its black plumage and bill contrasting with its conspicuous red face, throat and throat-pouch. The sexes appear similar although the female's casque is smaller and there is a blue patch in the centre of her red throat-pouch.

Ground hornbills occur widely through the Park, often in groups of up to eight birds. Although they can fly powerfully when required (and roost at night in trees), they are essentially terrestrial and are usually seen foraging on the ground for reptiles (including tortoises), frogs, snails, insects and small mammals. Unlike other hornbill species, the female does not seal herself into her nest during incubation.

LESSER STRIPED SWALLOW
Hirundo abyssinica
KLEINSTREEPSWAEL

The lesser striped swallow is one of the 12 swallow and martin species recorded from the Park. A common, breeding, intra-African migrant, it arrives in June and leaves again in March/April.

The lesser striped swallow is similar to the greater striped swallow (which also occurs in the Park) but is smaller, with the white throat and belly heavily streaked in black (as opposed to light black streaks in the greater striped swallow) and the ear-coverts chestnut-coloured (instead of white) like the crown. The lesser striped swallow's nest is a bowl-shaped mud chamber with a tubular entrance, and may be constructed on the underside of rock overhangs, the eaves of buildings or stout branches.

PHOTO ACCESS/LEX HES

CRESTED BARBET

BLACK-COLLARED BARBET

CRESTED BARBET
Trachyphonus vaillantii
KUIFKOPHOUTKAPPER

Barbets are small, thickset birds related to woodpeckers. They obtain their name from the distinctive 'beard' of feathers and bristles around the base of their stout, sharply pointed bills (the Latin word *barbatus* meaning bearded).

The crested barbet is the largest barbet in the region, with a bill- to tail-tip length of some 24 centimetres. It is easily recognised by its distinctive yellow and black plumage, with a broad black breast band. It is a noisy, conspicuous bird, usually occurring singly or in pairs, and is found in the Park in woodland habitats and often in rest-camps. The male's call is a loud, monotonous, unmusical trill like an alarm clock with the bell removed, which can be sustained for up to 30 seconds. The crested barbet spends a lot of time on the ground feeding on insects, worms, fruit and snails.

BLACK-COLLARED BARBET
Lybius torquatus
ROOIKOPHOUTKAPPER

The black-collared barbet is a very striking bird with its diagnostic bright-red (rarely yellow) face, throat and breast, broadly bordered in black over the hindcrown, nape and lower breast. Its back is greyish olive and the belly is a dull yellow. It is a widespread resident species in the Park, favouring woodland habitats. Breeding takes place in summer, the birds excavating a nest-hole in a tree-trunk or branch. Sometimes two pairs of birds may share a nest-hole. Their diet consists of fruit (especially figs) and various insects.

The call of the black-collared barbet is a distinctive duet which has been rendered in words as '*two-puddly, two-puddly...*' (or '*clean-collar, clean collar...*') repeated up to eight times in quick succession, with one bird singing the '*two*' and the other immediately answering '*puddly*'.

100

FORK-TAILED DRONGO

BLACK-HEADED ORIOLE

FORK-TAILED DRONGO

Dicrurus adsimilis

MIKSTERTBYVANGER

Two species of drongo occur in South Africa: the fork-tailed drongo and the square-tailed drongo. Both occur in the Park, but the square-tailed species is rarely encountered and then usually near stands of trees near rivers. The fork-tailed drongo on the other hand, is a widespread and common resident of the Park, occurring in savanna woodland, riverine vegetation and even around rest camps. Both species are entirely black with a metallic sheen to the feathers, but – as their names imply – the one has a deeply forked tail while the other has only a very slight notch.

The fork-tailed drongo is a pugnacious bird which will harass large birds of prey, small mammals, and even people if they should dare approach its nest. It occurs singly or in pairs and swoops from a perch at its (largely) insect prey.

BLACK-HEADED ORIOLE

Oriolus larvatus

SWARTKOPWIELEWAAL

Orioles are medium-sized, predominantly yellow birds with slightly curved bills. Three out of the four southern African species occur in the Park, and of these one of the most common is the black-headed oriole. It frequents woodland and riverine bush but is sometimes difficult to see as it keeps mostly to the tops of the taller trees. It usually occurs singly or in pairs and feeds on insects, fruit and nectar.

The black-headed oriole is distinctively coloured, with its bright, glossy black head, neck and upper breast, greenish-yellow back and bright-yellow underparts. It is highly vocal, particularly in the early morning, and has a wide repertoire of melodious liquid piping and bubbling notes.

Breeding takes place in early summer, and the nest is a deep cup of lichen, moss, grass and spider-web.

BLACK-EYED BULBUL   AFRICAN PIED WAGTAIL

BLACK-EYED BULBUL
Pycnonotus barbatus
SWARTOOGTIPTOL

Although they are shy, forest- and wood-dwelling birds, certain of South Africa's eight bulbul species have adapted to man's activities and occur in city parks and gardens. One of these is the black-eyed bulbul which occurs widespread throughout the Park, especially in the south, and is often seen at rest-camps and picnic-sites.

It is a smallish bird with a grey-brown back and wings, a dark-brown breast shading to a whitish belly, and a conspicuous lemon-yellow vent; its black head distinguishes it from the other four bulbul species in the Park. This restless, highly vocal bulbul with its liquid whistling 'wake-up Gregory' call, usually occurs in pairs or small groups and feeds on fruit and insects.

AFRICAN PIED WAGTAIL
Motacilla aguimp
BONTKWIKKIE

Five species occur in southern Africa, of which four can be found in the Kruger National Park. The most striking of these is the African pied wagtail, with its black upperparts, tail and breast-band, and contrasting white underparts, eyebrow, neck patch and wing-stripe. It occurs widely through Africa and is a resident breeding species in South Africa.

The African pied wagtail is found throughout the Park at rivers and large dams, where it can be observed walking briskly about, constantly wagging its tail up and down. It may be found in groups of a few to several dozen birds except during the breeding season – September to October – when it may be seen singly or in pairs.

LONG-TAILED SHRIKE

WHITE HELMET-SHRIKE

PHOTO ACCESS/LEX HES

PHOTO ACCESS/J.F. CARLYON

LONG-TAILED SHRIKE
Corvinella melanoleuca
LANGSTERTLAKSMAN

Shrikes are small- to medium-sized perch-ing birds with strong, hooked and toothed bills. They are bold, aggressive predators on insects and the smaller vertebrates, which are pounced on from a perch and caught on the ground. Their habit of impaling dead prey on thorns has led to them also being called 'butcher-birds'.

The long-tailed shrike is one of four shrike species known to occur in the Park, where it inhabits acacia savanna. Its whole plumage is black, except for a long white V on the lower back, a grey rump and some white on the wings. Its distinguishing fea-ture is its long tail, around 30 centimetres, which is more than twice as long as its body. It usually occurs in small groups.

WHITE HELMET-SHRIKE
Prionops plumatus
WITHELMLAKSMAN

The helmet-shrikes are a family of small, social shrikes with four representatives in southern Africa, three of which occur in the Kruger National Park. One of these is the white helmet-shrike, which is a common Park resident favouring woodland habitats. It is boldly pied in black and white. It has a grey crown with loose, bushy feathers which tend to project forward over the bill. Like others of the genus *Prionops*, it has a small but obvious ring of fleshy wattles around the eye, in this case coloured orange-yellow.

It is gregarious at all times, occurring in flocks of six to 20 birds, all co-operating in activities as divergent as nest-building and feeding of the young.

103

BRUBRU

SOUTHERN BOUBOU

BRUBRU

Nilaus afer

BONTROKLAKSMAN

This small bush-shrike occurs widespread throughout the Park, where it inhabits open woodland and acacia-veld. It is insectivorous and not often seen, living high in the canopies of trees where it gleans its prey from foliage and branches. It resembles the flycatchers of the genus *Batis*, but it is larger and has a thicker bill. It is mainly black above, mottled with white on the back and wings, and white below with bright chestnut on the flanks.

Like other arboreal bush-shrikes, the brubru is more often heard than seen; it calls continually, often in alternating duet. The male's call is a far-carrying, high-pitched trill which can be rendered as '*chuk-prrrreeee*' or '*chukchuk-prrrreeee*'.

SOUTHERN BOUBOU

Laniarius ferrugineus

SUIDELIKE WATERFISKAAL

Bush-shrikes are closely related to the true shrikes and there are 14 species of this exclusively African family in South Africa. The Park is host to 11 species of bush-shrike. One of these is the southern boubou which is named for one of its several calls, '*boo-boo*'. It is more often heard than seen and characteristically sings in duet, one bird transmitting one call, the other answering immediately with a different call, for example, '*boo-boo*'... '*whee-oo*'.

It has black upperparts with a white wing-bar, and whitish underparts flushed with rufous on the flanks. In the Park it is quite common in dense bush habitats, where it hunts among the undergrowth for insects, eggs and fledglings.

WATTLED STARLING BREEDING MALE

PETER PICKFORD

WATTLED STARLING

Creatophora cinerea

LELSPREEU

There are some 106 species of starlings world-wide, of which 12 occur in South Africa; two of these, the Indian myna and the European starling, are alien introductions from overseas. The Park is host to eight indigenous species.

One of these is the wattled starling, found throughout southern Africa in farmland, savanna and woodland. It is a summer nomad to the Park, particularly to the north of the Sabie River, and its numbers are highest during seasons of high rainfall. Like other starlings it is gregarious and it roosts and nests communally in trees in flocks of sometimes thousands strong.

The diet of the wattled starling is varied; it takes caterpillars, grasshoppers, swarming termites, worms, snails, offal (it frequents rubbish-pits and abattoirs), fruit and the nectar of flowering trees and aloes. It is also reputed to follow locust swarms closely and to breed near concentrations of young locusts. If the locusts move on too soon, the nests and young of the starling are deserted by the parents. The nest is a large untidy pile of sticks and grass and a clutch may contain between two and five eggs.

The wattled starling is about the size of a laughing dove. Breeding males are particularly conspicuous with their extraordinary black wattles projecting from the throat, forehead and crown, complemented by the yellow hindcrown, pale whitish-grey body and the black flight-feathers and tail. Outside the breeding season, the wattles and the yellow coloration of the crown disappear and the body colour becomes darker grey like the female's.

PLUM-COLOURED STARLING MALE

BURCHELL'S STARLING

PLUM-COLOURED STARLING
Cinnyricinclus leucogaster
WITBORSSPREEU

The plum-coloured starling is a common intra-African breeding migrant to the Kruger National Park, arriving in October and departing in March. It is strongly sexually dimorphic, that is the male and the female differ markedly in appearance. The male's upperparts, throat, breast and tail are iridescent violet-plum in colour, shot with bronze, while its underparts are white. The female, on the other hand, is thrush-like in appearance, being light-brown streaked with black above, and white heavily streaked with brown below.

They occur in pairs when breeding but are gregarious in small flocks at other times. They are normally seen feeding on fruit in trees, but will also take insects on occasion.

BURCHELL'S STARLING
Lamprotornis australis
GROOTGLANSSPREEU

Five of South Africa's 12 starling species are the so-called 'glossy' starlings of the genus *Lamprotornis*. These very striking birds are all characterized by having black plumage which is shot with a green, blue and purple metallic lustre.

Burchell's starling is typical of the group and is one of the largest, with a bill- to tail-tip length of up to 34 centimetres. It is glossy blue-green overall, with some purple, and has a dark ear-patch below the eye. The longish tail is shot with purple and barred with black.

It normally occurs in small groups but roosts communally in large noisy flocks. In the Kruger National Park it is restricted to the area south of the Olifants River.

GREATER BLUE-EARED STARLING

GLOSSY STARLING

GREATER BLUE-EARED STARLING

Lamprotornis chalybaeus

GROOT-BLOUOORGLANSSPREEU

Although the general colour of the greater blue eared starling is an iridescent blue-green, its ear-coverts are deep purple (almost blackish) and its belly and flanks are violet-blue. It has a bright-orange eye and its tail is of 'normal' length. (Burchell's starling has a dark brown eye and long tail.)

This highly coloured starling is widespread in the north of the Kruger National Park but also occurs along the western boundary in suitable localities and is frequently seen at Pretoriuskop, Skukuza and Tshokwane. It is found in pairs when breeding but is otherwise gregarious in large flocks. It forages on the ground for fruit, insects and seeds and often takes scraps from rest-camp tables.

GLOSSY STARLING

Lamprotornis nitens

KLEINGLANSSPREEU

The glossy starling itself is the most widespread of the five members of the 'glossy starling' group in South Africa and it is a common resident of the Kruger National Park, especially in the southern districts. It is similar in appearance to the greater blue-eared starling, both being metallic blue-green overall; the glossy starling lacks the dark ear-patch, however, its head and ear-coverts being a uniform metallic blue, while its belly and flanks are glossy-green, not violet-blue.

It occurs in pairs in the breeding season but is otherwise gregarious in small, loose parties of six to 10 birds. It forages both in trees and on the ground, feeding on insects, fruit and the nectar of aloes.

RED-WINGED STARLING FEMALE

RED-BILLED OXPECKER

RED-WINGED STARLING
Onychognathus morio
ROOIVLERKSPREEU

The male red-winged starling can be easily recognized with his overall glossy blue-black coloration and rich-chestnut wing-feathers (conspicuous in flight). The female is similar, but her head, upper breast and upper mantle are dark grey, streaked with blue-black.

This common resident of the Lowveld prefers rocky habitats and is found in such localities in patches down the length of the Park, especially along the eastern side. It is a noisy, gregarious bird, found in flocks of a few birds to hundreds except when it pairs off during the summer breeding season.

Fruit, insects, ticks, lizards and aloe nectar constitute its diet, and it forages both arboreally and on the ground.

RED-BILLED OXPECKER
Buphagus erythrorhynchus
ROOIBEKRENOSTERVOËL

The red-billed oxpecker is the more common of the two oxpecker species in the Kruger National Park and may be found throughout the savanna and bushveld areas in association with large herbivorous game animals. Both sexes have dark-brown upperparts, throat and breast, and creamy-buff underparts. The eyes are surrounded by a yellow wattle ring and the bill is entirely waxy red in colour.

This fascinating species has a heavy bill suited for removing ticks (its principal food) and other ectoparasites from the skin of tame animals. It is normally found in groups of two to six birds, favouring giraffe, buffalo and rhinoceros, but also foraging on kudu, sable, zebra and impala.

YELLOW-BILLED OXPECKER

ON GIRAFFE

MARICO SUNBIRD MALE

PHOTO ACCESS/PETER STEYN

AFRICAN IMAGES/DUNCAN BUTCHART

YELLOW-BILLED OXPECKER
Buphagus africanus
GEELBEKRENOSTERVOËL

The yellow-billed oxpecker is larger than the red-billed oxpecker, and is nowadays a rare species throughout southern Africa as a result of the eradication of game animals outside game reserves, and the reduction of ticks by cattle dipping. It had not been seen in the Park for years when, in 1980, there were two sightings between Shingwedzi and Punda Maria and in 1985 a nest was discovered. The yellow-billed oxpecker has since spread throughout the Park. While more common in the north, it is sporadically seen south of the Letaba River.

Distinguished from the red-billed oxpecker by its heavier bill, which is mostly yellow with a red tip, the yellow-billed oxpecker also takes ticks from large herbivores.

MARICO SUNBIRD
Nectarinia mariquensis
MARICOSUIKERBEK

Sunbirds are small birds with long, slim, decurved bills which feed on soft-bodied insects and nectar. They obtain nectar by clinging to or standing on a flower-head, and inserting their bills and long tubular tongues into the flowers, sometimes puncturing the flower at the base of the tube. There are at least five species in the Park.

The Marico sunbird is the most common sunbird species in the Park and is often seen in rest-camps feeding at flowers, but otherwise in acacia savanna and riverine forest. The male has a brilliant metallic-green head, breast and upperparts, with a blue breast-band shading to metallic-violet, a black belly, wings and tail, and a peacock-blue rump.

WHITE-BELLIED SUNBIRD MALE

SPOTTED-BACKED WEAVER BREEDING MALE

WHITE-BELLIED SUNBIRD
Nectarinia talatala
WITPENSSUIKERBEK

The female white-bellied sunbird has no iridescent coloration, being brownish-grey above and greyish-white below. The male, however, is strikingly colourful with head, throat and upperparts bright metallic-green, a dark metallic-purple breast-band, and a white belly. No other sunbird in the Park has a white belly.

This species occurs widespread through the Park in acacia savanna where it feeds on nectar from various flowers, particularly aloes and mistletoes. It also takes soft-bodied insects and spiders. Like other sunbirds, this active bird builds an oval, hanging nest using grass, fibre, dead leaves and other debris, bound with spider-web and lined within with soft plant-down and feathers.

SPOTTED-BACKED WEAVER
Ploceus cucullatus
BONTRUGWEWER

Seven species of the genus *Ploceus* – the 'true' weavers – occur in the Park. They are all primarily yellow in colour, and all except the spectacled weaver are gregarious colonial breeders. The males acquire a brightly-coloured plumage during the breeding season.

The spotted-backed weaver is typical of the group and is a common resident of the Park, especially in summer when it is frequently seen at rest-camps and along rivers. The breeding male is easily distinguished from other weavers by its yellow upperparts heavily spotted with black. Its underparts are yellow (as in other weavers) and it has a black face and throat; there is no black on the forehead or crown.

SPECTACLED WEAVER MALE

LESSER MASKED WEAVER BREEDING MALE

SPECTACLED WEAVER
Ploceus ocularis
BRILWEWER

The spectacled weaver is distinguished readily from other 'yellow' weavers by the black eye-stripe which is present in both sexes throughout the year. (In this species the male does not have a different eclipse plumage outside the breeding season.) The male may be distinguished from the female and from other weavers by its black 'bib' on throat and chin.

Preferring riverine forest and dense shrub habitats, it occurs throughout the Park in such localities, for example along the well-wooded Luvuvhu, Sabie and Crocodile rivers. Unlike most other weavers in the Park it is not a social species, and is usually seen singly or in pairs, foraging in the undergrowth for food.

LESSER MASKED WEAVER
Ploceus intermedius
KLEINGEELVINK

Both the masked and the lesser masked weaver occur in the Kruger National Park and may cause identification problems. The breeding males of both have yellowish-green upperparts and yellow underparts, with a black face and throat. Their distinguishing features are the colour of their eyes (red in the masked weaver and yellow in the lesser masked weaver) and the extent of the black plumage (which does not extend on to the top of the crown above the eye in the masked weaver, but does in the lesser masked weaver).

The lesser masked weaver is gregarious, but breeding colonies seldom contain more than 10 pairs. The oval nest has a short vertical entrance tube.

GOLDEN WEAVER BREEDING MALE

RED-HEADED WEAVER BREEDING MALE

GOLDEN WEAVER
Ploceus xanthops
GOUDWEWER

As in many other weaver species, the male golden weaver undergoes a seasonal plumage change. It is one of the largest of the weavers, and its yellow eyes and heavy bill distinguish it from the yellow weaver which is slightly smaller and has red eyes. The breeding male is golden-yellow below and golden-green above, moulting to lemon-yellow below and yellowish-green above outside the breeding season.

It is not particularly common in the Park, and has only been recorded from the Luvuvhu and Limpopo rivers and from around the confluence of the Olifants and Timbavati rivers. It prefers rank vegetation along streams and rivers where it feeds in small groups on insects, fruits and seeds.

RED-HEADED WEAVER
Anaplectes rubriceps
ROOIKOPWEWER

The breeding male of the red-headed weaver is one of the most distinctive of all weavers; its head, breast and upper back are brilliant scarlet, contrasting with the white belly, grey lower back and dusky wings edged in yellow. In non-breeding males and females the scarlet is replaced by dull orange above and pale yellow on the breast. The bill is red or orange-red.

This smallish weaver is usually seen singly or in pairs, foraging for insects and spiders, as well as seeds and fruit in the foliage of its woodland and bushveld habitat. It is a quiet, unobtrusive species and occurs throughout the Park in suitable habitat, usually not far from water. Breeding takes places from August to February.

RED-BILLED QUELEA RED BISHOP BREEDING MALE

RED-BILLED QUELEA
Quelea quelea
ROOIBEKKWELEA

The red-billed quelea is well known throughout Africa as a highly nomadic, extremely gregarious seed-eating pest of agricultural land. Its numbers can reach plague proportions, with flocks of hundreds of thousands of birds descending on grain-crops in synchronized waves, systematically stripping the plants of their seeds.

This small, finch-like bird occurs widely in the Kruger National Park, breeding there from January to March. It is a colonial breeder and nesting colonies may cover several hectares. The nests are woven by the males in thorn-trees (up to 500 nests per tree) or in reed-beds and are small, thin-walled, ball-shaped, grass-woven structures with a wide entrance.

RED BISHOP
Euplectes orix
ROOIVINK

Although bishops and widows are closely related enough to be placed in the same genus, *Euplectes*, all bishops have short tails at all times while the males of most widow species have long tails in the breeding season. Both groups, however, are strongly sexually dimorphic in the breeding season, when the males develop highly distinctive and brightly coloured plumage.

The red bishop is one of the most striking members of the genus, with the male developing brilliant orange-scarlet and black plumage during the breeding season, which is usually in the middle of summer in the Kruger National Park. The males are polygamous, with up to seven females each, and they inhabit reed-beds and marshy areas.

GOLDEN BISHOP: BREEDING MALE WITH FEMALE

WHITE-WINGED WIDOW BREEDING MALE

GOLDEN BISHOP
Euplectes afer
GOUDGEELVINK

The golden bishop is less common in the Park than the red bishop, but records do exist confirming its presence during summer in moist grassland habitats, vleis, seasonally flooded pans and in the rank, weedy vegetation bordering dams.

The golden bishop is gregarious at all times, sometimes occurring in flocks of hundreds of birds. The breeding plumage of the male is a combination of black underparts and brilliant yellow upperparts; females and non-breeding males are nondescript brownish birds by contrast. When the male displays, he fluffs his plumage like a gold and black ball, beats his wings so fast that they are almost invisible, and gives vent to a high-pitched buzzing display call.

WHITE-WINGED WIDOW
Euplectes albonotatus
WITVLERKFLAP

Like other bishops and widows of the genus *Euplectes*, the white-winged widow is highly sexually dimorphic, that is the males and females are markedly different in appearance, but only in the breeding season. The breeding male is black overall, with a brilliant yellow patch at the bend of the wing, and white primary wing-coverts which show up as a conspicuous flash in flight. This white patch distinguishes it from the similar yellow-rumped widow which also occurs in the Park. Females and non-breeding males are a nondescript brown above and whitish-buff below.

It is a gregarious species and feeds on seeds, insects and the nectar of aloes. The males may have up to four females each.

N. BRICKELL

PIN-TAILED WHYDAH BREEDING MALE

N. BRICKELL

PARADISE WHYDAH BREEDING MALE

PIN-TAILED WHYDAH

Vidua macroura

KONINGROOIBEK

Whydahs are 'brood parasites', laying their eggs in the nests of other birds, especially waxbills. In several whydah species, the four central tail-feathers of the breeding males are greatly elongated.

The pin-tailed whydah is typical of the group; the breeding male has distinctive black-and-white plumage, a brilliant red bill and a streaming black tail made up of four long and narrow tail-feathers. Males are polygamous and may acquire up to six females each. The females lay their eggs in the nests of several host species, the common waxbill being the favourite. They are summer-breeding visitors to the Park and occur in small flocks of up to 30 birds in lightly wooded savanna or grassland.

PARADISE WHYDAH

Vidua paradisea

GEWONE PARADYSVINK

The breeding male of this species is unmistakable with his resplendent long black tail, set off by the chestnut-brown breast and broad ochre collar around the hindneck. The inner two tail feathers are very broad and taper off into long filaments; the next pair are broad, extremely long and taper gradually to a point. Females and non-breeding males are comparatively drab with tails of normal length.

The paradise whydah is common and widespread in the Kruger National Park, favouring acacia savanna and dry open woodland. It is a brood parasite, the females laying their eggs in the nests of the melba finch, one to three eggs per nest and up to 22 eggs per female per season.

W. R. BRANCH

W. R. BRANCH

LEOPARD TORTOISE

SERRATED TERRAPIN

LEOPARD TORTOISE

Geochelone pardalis
BERGSKILPAD

SERRATED TERRAPIN

Pelusios sinuatus
GROOT WATERSKILPAD

Two of South Africa's 11 land tortoise species and three of its five terrapins occur in the Kruger National Park. Although they are all typical chelonians and have a bony horn-covered shell as protective armour, tortoises and terrapins have pursued different evolutionary courses.

South African land tortoises are 'hidden-necked' tortoises, that is, they draw the neck in with a vertical bend, pulling the forelegs in afterwards to hide the head completely. The region's terrapins, however, are 'side-necked' tortoises; they pull the neck in sideways bringing the head under the shell but leaving it exposed to view. To counter this problem, some of the terrapin species

(including two of the three in the Park) have evolved a hinge on the under-shell, which allows the front of the under-shell to be pulled up like a drawbridge to hide the head and legs completely.

The leopard tortoise is the largest of the region's tortoise species, with a maximum shell length of 50 centimetres. It is widely distributed through the Park. It is a vegetarian. In spring, the females may lay several clutches of between five and 30 eggs which hatch out eight to 13 months later. Each year veld fires take their toll of tortoises, as do a wide range of predators.

The serrated terrapin inhabits all the perennial rivers in the Park as well as the more permanent water-holes and dams. It may often be seen basking in the sun and can be recognized by its domed shell and the serrations of the edge of its shell at the back. It is essentially carnivorous and congregates in large numbers at the decaying carcasses of animals caught by crocodiles, which, ironically, are its major enemy.

NILE CROCODILE

NILE CROCODILE

Crocodylus niloticus
NYLKROKODIL

While it is difficult to obtain authenticated records for any crocodile species anywhere in the world, crocodile-hunters as a rule having more fertile imaginations than fishermen, it seems that the Nile crocodile of Africa could claim to be the third-largest crocodilian with apparently valid lengths of about 6,5 metres on record.

These are extraordinary specimens, however, and an average-sized adult crocodile in the Kruger National Park will attain a length of only 3,6 to 3,9 metres. Extremely large individuals in the Olifants and Luvuvhu rivers, however, have been measured at over 4,5 metres.

Crocodiles occur in all the perennial and many of the seasonal rivers of the Park, as well as in dams and water-holes. The Olifants and Luvuvhu rivers, which are discoloured by silt almost throughout the year, carry a larger population than the rivers with clear water. Murky waters are preferred habitat, as they provide ideal camouflage for the stalking of prey.

They prey on a wide range of vertebrate animals, from catfish and terrapins to full-grown lions, buffalo and zebra which are often caught by the nose while drinking at the water's edge. The crocodile's respiratory system is well adapted for predation in an aquatic environment: the external nostrils have 'valves' which close when it submerges and there is also a valve-like glottis in the throat which allows the crocodile to hold its prey in its jaws below water without swallowing water or flooding the lungs.

Female crocodiles lay between 25 and 75 eggs above water level in sand or sandy soil. The nests are guarded by the female for the three-month incubation period and when the eggs hatch, she carries the babies in her mouth to a nursery area and continues to look after them for the crucial first three or four months.

BOOMSLANG

BLACK MAMBA

BOOMSLANG
Dispholidus typus
BOOMSLANG

The snake family Colubridae contains nearly two-thirds of the world's 3 000 snake species, most of them harmless to man. Certain species, however, are endowed with poison-glands and are known as back-fanged snakes because the enlarged grooved teeth modified to conduct venom are usually situated midway along the upper jaw, just below the eye.

The boomslang is one such species, found in wooded habitats throughout the Park. It is an agile tree-dwelling snake which preys upon chamaeleons, small birds, mice and frogs. Although it is widely feared because of its extremely toxic venom, it is non-aggressive and is really dangerous only to foolhardy snake-collectors.

BLACK MAMBA
Dendroaspis polylepis
SWARTMAMBA

The family Elapidae, of which the black mamba is a member, is a large group of venomous snakes, all of which possess a highly specialized poison apparatus. This consists of a pair (rarely two pairs) of rigid fangs near the front of the upper jaw, which may be deeply grooved or tubular for the transport of venom to the snake's victim. The venom is highly neurotoxic, causing paralysis of the nervous system.

In the Park the black mamba is not uncommon, occurring in the lower-lying, drier and more open bush country. It preys upon dassies, rodents and small birds. With its unpredictable temperament, its aggress-iveness, its speed and its size, it is perhaps the most feared snake of the bushveld.

EGYPTIAN COBRA

MOZAMBIQUE SPITTING COBRA

EGYPTIAN COBRA

Naja haje

EGIPTIESE KOBRA

The Egyptian cobra is the less common of the two cobra species occurring in the Kruger National Park, although it is widely distributed in suitable habitat in dry open savanna, often far from water. It is larger than the Mozambique spitting cobra, normally attaining a length of between 1,5 and 2 metres but sometimes up to 3 metres. Although not normally aggressive, it can rear up some 45 to 60 centimetres from the ground when threatened, spreading the typical cobra hood which may be as much as 12,5 centimetres across.

The diet of the Egyptian cobra consists of rodents, lizards, snakes, frogs, birds and birds' eggs although its favourite prey items appear to be toads. It hunts mostly at night.

MOZAMBIQUE SPITTING COBRA

Naja mossambica

MOSAMBIEK-SPOEGKOBRA

This snake is the common cobra species of the Transvaal Lowveld and the more abundant of the two cobra species of the Park. It is widely distributed through the Park in savanna habitats. Unlike the Egyptian cobra, the spitting cobra appears to prefer localities near water and will readily take refuge in water when disturbed.

It is considered to be the second most dangerous snake in Africa after the black mamba, as it can either kill a potential aggressor with its bite or cause blindness by 'spitting' its neurotoxic venom into the eyes; this is performed with accuracy and speed over distances of up to four metres and unless the poison is washed out immediately, permanent blindness can result.

AFRICAN ROCK-PYTHON

PUFF-ADDER

AFRICAN ROCK-PYTHON
Python sebae
LUISLANG

PUFF-ADDER
Bitis arietans
POFADDER

The longest snakes in the world belong to the family Boidae, which includes the pythons, boas and the anaconda. The African rock-python is considered to be the world's third-largest snake, after the South American anaconda and the Asian reticulated python, with a verified measurement of 9,1 metres from East Africa. An average South African python, however, will measure only three or four metres.

The python is widespread in the Park, favouring rocky, well-wooded valleys and reed-beds, never far from water. Most active at night, the python seeks prey up to the size of an impala, seizing the victim with its teeth and causing suffocation by coiling around it and constricting.

The 'true' adders, the vipers of the Old World have the most sophisticated poison apparatus of all snakes; their long, recurved, tubular fangs fold back against the roof of the mouth and swing forward to an erect position when the mouth is opened to strike. The venom is injected through the fang deep into the victim.

The puff-adder is a typical viper and is common and widespread throughout the Park. It is a fat, sluggish snake, normally about a metre in length, which relies on its cryptic coloration to escape notice. The puff-adder does not pursue its prey but ambushes it from a concealed position; for this reason it is dangerous to humans as it can be accidentally trodden upon.

PHOTO ACCESS/J&B PHOTOGRAPHERS

PHOTO ACCESS/PETER STEYN

ROCK LEGUAAN

WATER LEGUAAN

ROCK LEGUAAN

Varanus exanthematicus

VELDLIKKEWAAN

The monitor lizards of the genus *Varanus* include the largest lizards in the world. The length record (over 4,5 metres) is held by the Salvadori monitor of Papua New Guinea, and the size record (over three metres with a mass of 100 kilograms) by the Komodo 'dragon' of Indonesia. The two monitors in South Africa are known as leguaans, and both occur in the Park

The rock leguaan is a stout, thickset, dark grey-brown lizard up to 1,3 metres long with wide transverse bands of yellowish-grey along its body. It is not at home in water, and is mainly terrestrial although it can climb trees. It occurs throughout the Park in open bush and savanna habitats and lives on small vertebrates and insects.

WATER LEGUAAN

Varanus niloticus

WATERLIKKEWAAN

The water leguaan (or Nile monitor) is more slender than the rock leguaan and can attain greater lengths, sometimes over two metres. It is confined to the vicinity of permanent water and in the Kruger National Park may be found along all perennial rivers as well as at dams and water-holes. It is usually dark olive-brown above, with narrow, broken transverse bands of yellow along the body and tail.

During the day they bask in the sun near water; if disturbed they plunge into the water and swim off swiftly, moving with sideways sweeps of the laterally compressed tail. Their diet consists largely of crabs and mussels but they also take small mammals and birds, fish, snails and insects.

CHECKLIST AND INDEX TO ENGLISH NAMES

Below is an alphabetical index of the more common (or more visible) mammals, birds and reptiles you can expect to see during your visit to the Kruger National Park, which are illustrated and described in this book.

The index is provided with a series of boxes and may also be used as a checklist. Record all the species you see on this trip by ticking off the first of the boxes per species entry; the other boxes can be used on future visits to the Park. In this way you can compare the relative viewing success of each visit.

MAMMALS

Antelope, roan 23	Jackal, black-backed 28
sable 22	Klipspringer 24
Baboon, chacma 45	Kudu 15
Badger, honey- 42	Leopard 32
Bat, Egyptian slit-faced 50	Lion 31
Sundevall's leaf-nosed 51	Mongoose, banded 40
Wahlberg's epauletted fruit- 50	dwarf 41
Buffalo, Cape 13	white-tailed 39
Bushbaby, lesser 44	Monkey, vervet 46
thick-tailed 44	Nyala 14
Bushbuck 16	Otter, Cape clawless 43
Caracal 34	Pangolin 47
Cheetah 30	Porcupine 48
Civet 37	Reedbuck 19
Dassie, rock 49	Rhinoceros, black 6
Dog, wild 29	white 7
Duiker, common 24	Serval 35
Elephant, African 8	Squirrel, tree- 48
Genet, large-spotted 38	Steenbok 25
small-spotted 38	Tsessebe 21
Giraffe 12	Warthog 11
Grysbok, Sharpe's 26	Waterbuck 18
Hare, scrub- 49	Wildcat, African 36
Hippopotamus 10	Wildebeest, blue 20
Hyaena, spotted 27	Zebra, Burchell's 9
Impala 17	

BIRDS

☐ Barbet, black-collared 100
☐ crested 100
☐ Bateleur 66
☐ Bee-eater, carmine 93
☐ European 94
☐ little 95
☐ white-fronted 94
☐ Bishop, golden 114
☐ red 113
☐ Boubou, southern 104
☐ Brubru 104
☐ Bulbul, black-eyed 102
☐ Bustard, kori 74
☐ Coucal, Burchell's 83
☐ Crake, black 73
☐ Cuckoo, diederik 84
☐ Klaas's 84
☐ Darter 52
☐ Dikkop, spotted 77
☐ water 78
☐ Dove, Cape turtle 79
☐ green-spotted 80
☐ laughing 80
☐ mourning 79
☐ Drongo, fork-tailed 101
☐ Duck, knob-billed 60
☐ white-faced 59
☐ Eagle, African fish- 67
☐ African hawk 65
☐ brown snake- 66
☐ martial 65
☐ tawny 64
☐ Wahlberg's 64
☐ Egret, cattle 54
☐ Finfoot, African 73
☐ Francolin, coqui 70
☐ crested 70
☐ Natal 71
☐ Swainson's 71

☐ Goose, Egyptian 60
☐ spur-winged 61
☐ Goshawk, dark chanting 68
☐ little banded 67
☐ Guinea-fowl, crested 72
☐ helmeted 72
☐ Gymnogene 68
☐ Hamerkop 55
☐ Heron, goliath 53
☐ green-backed 54
☐ grey 53
☐ Hoopoe 96
☐ Hornbill, grey 97
☐ ground 99
☐ red-billed 98
☐ trumpeter 97
☐ yellow-billed 98
☐ Ibis, hadeda 59
☐ Jacana, African 75
☐ Kingfisher, brown-hooded 92
☐ giant 90
☐ half-collared 91
☐ malachite 91
☐ pied 90
☐ striped 93
☐ woodland 92
☐ Kite, black 69
☐ black-shouldered 69
☐ yellow-billed 69
☐ Korhaan, black-bellied 74
☐ red-crested 75
☐ Lourie, grey 82
☐ purple-crested 82
☐ Mousebird, red-faced 89
☐ speckled 89
☐ Nightjar, fiery-necked 88
☐ Mozambique 88
☐ Oriole, black-headed 101
☐ Ostrich 52

☐☐☐☐ Owl, barn 85
☐☐☐☐   giant eagle- 87
☐☐☐☐   marsh 85
☐☐☐☐   pearl-spotted 86
☐☐☐☐   scops 86
☐☐☐☐   spotted eagle- 87
☐☐☐☐ Oxpecker, red-billed 108
☐☐☐☐   yellow-billed 109
☐☐☐☐ Parrot, brown-headed 81
☐☐☐☐   Cape 81
☐☐☐☐ Plover, blacksmith 76
☐☐☐☐   crowned 77
☐☐☐☐   three-banded 76
☐☐☐☐ Quelea, red-billed 113
☐☐☐☐ Roller, European 95
☐☐☐☐   lilac-breasted 96
☐☐☐☐ Sandgrouse, double-banded 78
☐☐☐☐ Secretary-bird 61
☐☐☐☐ Shrike, long-tailed 103
☐☐☐☐   white helmet- 103
☐☐☐☐ Starling, Burchell's 106
☐☐☐☐   glossy 107
☐☐☐☐   greater blue-eared 107
☐☐☐☐   plum-coloured 106
☐☐☐☐   red-winged 108
☐☐☐☐   wattled 105
☐☐☐☐ Stork, Abdim's 57
☐☐☐☐   black 56
☐☐☐☐   marabou 55
☐☐☐☐   open-billed 57
☐☐☐☐   saddle-billed 58
☐☐☐☐   white 56
☐☐☐☐ Sunbird, Marico 109
☐☐☐☐   white-bellied 110
☐☐☐☐ Swallow, lesser striped 99
☐☐☐☐ Vulture, Cape 63
☐☐☐☐   hooded 62
☐☐☐☐   lappet-faced 63
☐☐☐☐   white-backed 62
☐☐☐☐ Wagtail, African pied 102
☐☐☐☐ Weaver, golden 112

☐☐☐☐   lesser masked 111
☐☐☐☐   red-headed 112
☐☐☐☐   spectacled 111
☐☐☐☐   spotted-backed 110
☐☐☐☐ Whydah, paradise 115
☐☐☐☐   pin-tailed 115
☐☐☐☐ Widow, white-winged 114

REPTILES

☐☐☐☐ Adder, puff- 120
☐☐☐☐ Boomslang 118
☐☐☐☐ Cobra, Egyptian 119
☐☐☐☐   Mozambique spitting 119
☐☐☐☐ Crocodile, Nile 117
☐☐☐☐ Leguaan, rock 121
☐☐☐☐   water 121
☐☐☐☐ Mamba, black 118
☐☐☐☐ Python, African rock- 120
☐☐☐☐ Terrapin, serrated 116
☐☐☐☐ Tortoise, leopard 116